The Accounting Game

Basic Accounting Fresh
from the Lemonade Stand

Judith Orloff
and Darrell Mullis

 SOURCEBOOKS, INC.®
NAPERVILLE, ILLINOIS

Published by Sourcebooks
P.O. Box 4410, Naperville, Illinois 60567
(630) 961-3900
FAX: (630) 961-2168
www.sourcebooks.com

Library of Congress Cataloging-in-Publication Data
Mullis, Darrell.
The accounting game: Basic accountinf fresh from the lemonade stand
Darrell Mullis, Judith Orloff.
    p.   cm.
Produced by Educational Discoveries.
ISBN 1-57071-396-0 (alk. paper)
    1. Accounting.   I. Orloff, Judith Handler. II. Educational Discoveries (Firm)
III. Title.
HF5635.M953   1998
657—dc21   98-17214
                                                  CIP

Printed and bound in the United States of America.

WA 20 19 18 17 16 15 14 13 12 11

TABLE OF CONTENTS

INTRODUCTION

How do people really learn? The answers and theories are endless. They include ideas ranging from genetic imprinting to osmosis and modeling and emotional intelligence. Brain research is voluminous as we enter the 21st century.

For now, though, please ask yourself: How do I learn?

Isn't that an interesting question? And, what do you learn? Do you learn information from reading, watching videos, using computers? Can you learn "people skills" without interacting with other people? Can you change behavior without a model of what the ideal behavior should look like? Feel like? Are there people you meet in your daily travels that you want to emulate? Do you emulate them? How does it work? Can you remember the words of the songs from childhood, but not the ones you listened to last week or even this morning? Questions and questions. More than any other thought process, questions help us learn.

Remember what we heard about a baby's first year of life? Babies learn more in that year than in all the years combined afterwards. Yet, in that first year, babies cannot pose questions in the way they will once they learn language. So, how do babies learn? And what can we take away from that to help adults learn more quickly, retain new information longer, and apply it immediately in their lives?

So, what does this have to do with you and this book? Good question.

The Accounting Game is written in a way that creates a specific learning experience for you as it teaches you the basic skills of accounting. We call the learning method accelerative learning. What do you think that means? It is a learning methodology that uses all of your senses as well as your emotions and your critical thinking skills. If you can remember your kindergarten or elementary school classrooms, you will see many colored maps, letters and numbers, bold (even raw) drawings by each child, etc. You learned the alphabet by singing. You learned the multiplication tables by saying them out loud with each other. You laughed a lot. You were creative.

Then, how you were taught began to change when you entered middle school or high school. Learning became more lecture, more black and white, more rote. You studied before tests and probably did well or maybe not. Yet, for all the endless homework and "cramming," most of the information you learned in high school you don't remember now. That's because it went into your short-term memory so that you could pass the tests and move on to the next grade.

Yet, look at all the things you remember from early childhood! While in elementary school, much of the information you learned went directly to your long-term memory, because it was peppered with music, color, movement, smells, emotional experiences, and lots of play and fun.

The methodology we use in this book in many ways parallels how you learned in grade school. We do this by accessing the part of your brain where long-term memory lives. Now, the way to reach your long-term memory has to include emotion, because they reside in the same place in your brain—the limbic region.

The truth is, because of the way we humans learn, we have to discover something ourselves to really learn it. This book is designed so you make dozens of discoveries. In short, you will learn a college semester's worth of accounting in the time it takes you to interact with this book.

This is quite a reversal, because business people and students have over the years found the subject of accounting quite difficult to master. Many have simply given up in frustration, others have decided to leave accounting to the "experts." This book is for all of you who have hated accounting, had difficulty learning it, or ever thought you didn't really "get it."

We think that most attempts to teach accounting fail because of too much attention to details and a failure to present the big picture framework of how it all works and fits together. In this book, we promise not to overburden you with details and to focus on what are really the key concepts of accounting that any businessperson needs to know.

You will learn the structure and purpose of the three primary financial statements—the balance sheet, the income statement, and the cash flow statement. You will learn how these fit together and their interrelationships. You will also learn the basic language of business—concepts like cost of goods sold, expenses, bad debts, accrual vs. cash methods of accounting, FIFO and LIFO, capitalizing vs. expensing, depreciation, and the difference between cash and profit.

Our promise is that you will get all this information in a fun and easy way that allows you to participate, interact, and discover all that you need to know. Many people need to have understanding and confidence in working with financial concepts, but are not ever going to be doing accounting details. If that is you, then this book fits that need, too. It is set up so that you can actually do financial statements as you are learning them. We invite you to "play the game" as you interact with this book.

Understanding all this information is nice, but what do you do with it? The final chapter will give you some tools for analyzing financial information and making better decisions for your company and your career.

As mentioned, the information in this program has been developed by Educational Discoveries, Inc. since the early 1980s in a one-day seminar, The Accounting Game™. The program was originally created by Marshall Thurber at the Burklyn Business School in the late 1970s. Nancy Maresh, a student at Marshall's school, then took the program and developed The Accounting Game seminar. We offer our heartfelt thanks for their original genius and commitment to bringing this extraordinary program to life. We also want to thank all of the somewhere between 75,000 and 100,000 people who have attended our public and private seminars for the fun they have been and for the insights and suggestions that have helped us improve the teaching of this information.

The Accounting Game is now offered in private seminars by MOHR Learning, a division of Provart, the parent company of Educational Discoveries, Inc. The Accounting Game continues to be the most successful financial seminar in the world.

So, enjoy! Because if you enjoy this book, you'll learn more in a brief time than you ever imagined possible.

Judith Orloff and Darrell Mullis
February 2001

PRE-TEST

1. Which one of the following items is not found on a Balance Sheet?

    A. Cash   B. Gross Profit

    C. Assets   D. Liabilities

2. Which accounting system most accurately reflects profitability?

    A. Cash Accounting   B. Flow of Funds Accounting

    C. Accrual Accounting

3. An account receivable is:

    A. an Asset   B. Owner's Equity

    C. a Liability

4. Which of the following is most important to the daily operations of a business?

    A. Assets   B. Retained Earnings

    C. Cash

5. When people speak about the bottom line, they are referring to:

    A. Net Profit   B. Gross Margin

    C. Gross Profit

6. A prepaid expense is:

    A. an Asset   B. Owner's Equity

    C. a Liability

7. Is LIFO/FIFO a method of:

    A. Inventory Evaluation   B. Profit Ratio

    C. Financing

8. Which would you find on an Income Statement?

    A. Expense   B. Fixed Asset

    C. Liability

9. Which of the following expenses does not affect your cash position in running a business:

    A. Lease Expense   B. Advertising Expense

    C. Depreciation Expense

10. Which of the following is a basic accounting equation:

    A. Net Worth = Assets + Profits

    B. Gross Profit - Sales = Gross Profit Margin

    C. Assets = Liabilities + Owner's Equity

CHAPTER 1

Remember how you learned to make money as a kid?

There was baby-sitting and delivering newspapers. Shoveling snow off the neighbors' sidewalk and driveway. Mowing lawns and taking care of other people's pets and plants when they went on vacation.

There is one business which, chances are, almost every kid tries at least once in his or her life. A tried and true operation as American as baseball and Mom's apple pie.

The Lemonade Stand.

It's this world of childhood, of lemonade stands and sunny days that we use in *The Accounting Game*. It's hand-made signs and scraps of lumber turned into a humble yet proud establishment. It's when saving up enough of your own money for a bike or a piece of sports equipment or horseback-riding lessons seemed the most important goal in the world. It's when you had your first inkling about money, and wished you understood everything you needed to know about it.

Now is your chance to go back, and learn what you need to know about the language of business, which goes by the name of Accounting.

So, find a quiet space and relax. Read a paragraph of the italicized passage below, then close your eyes and visualize what you've just read. When you're ready, go on to the next section, and the next...

Let yourself slowly go back in time...

Let's go back, all the way back to grade school. Picture yourself somewhere between five to ten years old. Let yourself remember what your childhood grade school looked like. If you went to more than one school, just pick out your favorite.

It's the last day of school. The sun is streaming through the classroom window. You can't wait for the final bell to ring one last time—then you'll be free! Free to run out the door with all your friends!

You're young and safe and eager. Everything is possible. You feel creative, curious, and excited, and know your success in life is absolutely assured.

Let this picture settle into your mind. Take a deep breath. Enjoy it.

The final school bell rings. You tell your teacher to have a good summer, and you rush out the door. It's so warm and wonderful outside! The sky is blue and you look up and see a few white, puffy, clouds decorating the view like a happy cartoon.

Kids are laughing. Lawnmowers are buzzing. Birds are chirping.

You can smell fresh cut grass and the scent of flowers.

You feel great.

You reach home and go inside. Since it's a special day, your mom or dad is home to meet you.

You're hot and excited, so you say, "What's to drink?"

And your mom or dad replies, "You're in luck! I just bought some lemons and some sugar so let's make some fresh-squeezed lemonade."

You get out a great big pitcher, fill it with water and ice, squeeze up some lemons, measure out the sugar, and mix up a batch of great tasting lemonade.

This is going to be one fun summer!

Take a moment and let this thought settle. Take a deep breath.

You take your drink outside and sit under your favorite tree. The lemonade tastes out of this world!

Then it hits you—people will pay good money for lemonade like this!

Ready? Good!

In the garage is the stuff you need to make a lemonade stand: two wooden fruit crates turned on their ends, some old cans of paint and brushes, a hammer and some nails. You take an hour or two to put your stand together. It's fun working with your hands and watching something of your own devising take shape. When you finish, you take a close look at your new place of business. If there's a finer lemonade stand in the world, you sure haven't seen it!

Here's your very own lemonade stand. Find some markers or stickers, and go ahead and decorate it, if you wish. Make it distinctively your own.

Now that your place of business is ready, you need a product—and that takes money! You run to your bedroom and shake out all the quarters and nickels and dimes from your piggy bank.

It adds up to FIVE DOLLARS!

You transfer the money to the closest equivalent you can find to a bulletproof, x-ray proof, robber proof, impossible-to-open safety deposit apparatus—an old cigar box your uncle was about to throw out.

You don't want to mess with all those coins, so your mom or dad graciously exchanges all of them for five, crisp one-dollar bills. The five dollars go into the cigar box bank for safe-keeping. In case anyone doesn't know the cigar box is off-limits, you take a marker and write on it:

PRIVATE PROPERTY!
KEEP OUT(OR DIE)!

Okay, your money is safe. What do we call those five one-dollar bills? *CASH!*

And what color is cash? *Green!*

Now that you're going to be rich, how are you going to keep track of the hundreds—no, millions! BILLIONS!—of dollars you're going to make selling lemonade? You need some paper and a pencil, for sure. You need some way to keep a record of what money goes in and out of your business. This record keeping is what accounting is all about.

You know enough about the world to know that one way grownups keep track of numbers is to keep score—like in baseball or golf, or whether your mom or dad last cleaned up after the dog in the back yard.

You decide to create a scorecard for your business.

Your scorecard allows you to keep track of things happening in your business. To better understand how money flows in and out of a business, though, we need a scorecard that shows two things: WHAT WE HAVE and WHO OWNS IT. Which means we need to draw a line down the middle of the scorecard. On the left side you'll track things and stuff you have and use in your business. On the right side you'll track who owns that stuff. So, your scorecard looks like this:

WHAT WE HAVE	WHO OWNS IT

The left side represents WHAT WE HAVE.

The right side of our scoreboard represents WHO OWNS IT.

Now that we have a proper scorecard, let's back up a moment. You start the business with some Cash, specifically five dollars.

Who has it?

You're right—you do! And, no doubt, you had to scrimp and save and keep your room clean and remind your parents a bunch of times to remember that the tooth fairy *always* leaves you some money when you lose a tooth. You worked hard for that five bucks! It's yours and nobody else's. Which means that it goes on the left side of the scorecard, as $5 in Cash. But it also goes on the right side since you own the $5. But what will you call this $5?

The whole idea is to invest the five bucks in your lemonade stand. Right?

So, what should we call the money that you originally shook from the piggy bank to invest in the lemonade stand?

How about "ORIGINAL INVESTMENT"?

Who owns the Original investment? You, as the owner, do. So it goes on the right side of our scorecard.

Let's write in what's happened, so far. Enter the five dollars in Cash on the left side and enter the five dollars in Original Investment on the right side. Next, enter the totals on the last line of each side.

Notice anything about the two sides?

They're equal. The left side equals the right side.

You now know an important rule about this financial scorecard. The left side will always, ALWAYS equal the right side!

Repeat this rule, please. Tape it to your forehead. Put it under your pillow at night, so you will remember it in your sleep:

THE LEFT SIDE ALWAYS EQUALS THE RIGHT SIDE!

So far, so good. The weather is great outside and you're ready to rock and roll! You can close your eyes and see the customers lining up around the block to sample your great tasting lemonade…until you realize that starting a lemonade stand will cost more than the original investment of five dollars because you have to buy stuff to make your lemonade.

Who is most kids' personal banker?

Right, Mom and Dad.

So you go to one of them (you know which one is more likely to say yes), and you say, "Here's your chance to teach me the real value of a dollar. Here's your chance to invest in a business sure to make lots of money. Here's your chance to help a budding billionaire. Here's your chance to keep me out of your hair until dinnertime!"

One of the reasons works, and Mom and Dad fork over TEN DOLLARS.

You're halfway out the door when Mom calls, "Hey, that ten dollars isn't a gift! It's a loan!"

You stop short. "A loan?" you repeat, making the word sound as disappointing as possible. "What's the matter? Don't you love me?"

"Nice Try," Mom says. This is all part of teaching you something about the real world. Okay, you still have the money, even after Mom makes you sign a piece of paper that says "IOU" at the top.

Still, the ten dollars is yours to use, so you can add it to your Cash under What We Have.

But you also owe it to Mom. So, since you don't, in fact, "own" the ten dollars, we need to create a new category on the right side (Who Owns It) of the scorecard. You have, in fact, just signed a "note" that is "payable" to your mom. Businesses have a name for an IOU. It's called Notes Payable. Go ahead and record these transactions.

WHAT WE HAVE		WHO OWNS IT	
CASH		NOTES PAYABLE	
		ORIGINAL INVESTMENT	
TOTAL		TOTAL	

So, we have the left side which represents what you have and use. And what do you have? Cash.

And how much cash so far? Fifteen dollars.

Businesses have a name for the WHAT WE HAVE. Do you know it? Assets.

So, from now on, we'll use Assets as our heading for the left side.

On the right side, who owns that cash? You own five and your bankers (Mom and Dad) own how much? Ten.

Since there are two owners on the right half, we will draw a horizontal line that divides the right side into two parts. The upper right side represents the people that the business owes money to…or to whom you are LIABLE. Are you going to have to pay back the ten dollars to Mom or Dad? (You'd better, if you want to see your next birthday!) So, are you liable to them for $10? Yes. Which is why, from now on, we'll label the top part of the right side, LIABILITIES. Notice we will use the color pink for liabilities.

The lower right side represents the portion of the business you own; right now, that is your Original Investment. What do some people call the part of the business owned by the owners? Make a check mark by the answer below. (Hint: there may be more than one answer.)

- ☐ Equity
- ☐ Owner's Equity
- ☐ Stockholders' Equity
- ☐ Net Worth

Did you make a check in front of all of the above? You should, because they're all the same thing. For our sake, we're going to call this lower right side, Owner's Equity, and represent it with the color black.

So, the right side has two parts: Liabilities (what you owe others) and Owner's Equity (what's yours).

Remember we said the left side always equals the right side? Well, here's the next accounting rule to remember:

Assets = Liabilities + Owner's Equity

Repeat this equation. Write it on the palm of your hand. Put it under a magnet on the fridge. Program it as your computer screensaver.

Here's your scorecard again, with the proper accounting terms.

ASSETS		LIABILITIES	
CASH	$15.00	NOTES PAYABLE	$10.00
		OWNER'S EQUITY	
		ORIGINAL INVESTMENT	$5.00
TOTAL ASSETS	$15.00	TOTAL LIABILITIES & OWNER'S EQUITY	$15.00

Before moving on—does the left side still equal the right side? *It should. Always! Always! Always!*

You're doing great. And, hopefully, you're having fun. You're making discoveries, maybe seeing things clearly for the first time.

What's a good way to capture such a beautiful moment? How about by taking a snapshot.

A BALANCE SHEET IS A SNAPSHOT IN TIME.

What period of time does a snapshot record? Check one:

◻ A moment

◻ Longer than a moment

The answer is: A MOMENT. Snapshots give us an image of where we are right NOW. This scorecard is like a snapshot. It gives us an image, frozen at a particular moment, of a business's financial position—what you have and where it came from. So, this scorecard shows a moment in time, and the two sides are equal—or, as they say, "in balance." So, from now on, let's call this scorecard...

A BALANCE SHEET!

But, for the moment, enough of this philosophical stuff about time and nitpicking over words—we're here to start a lemonade stand!

Having the money to start your business, you tell your mom and dad that you're biking to the store for supplies. The money in your pocket or pack feels enormous! You bike as fast as you can, so you can spend the money before you somehow lose it. Or before any robber is stupid enough to even try and catch you on your fleeting bike.

You make it to your neighborhood grocery store. It's run by Mr. Pappy Parker, whom everyone calls "Pappy." He has a large friendly face and a big nose. His eyes are blue, his eyebrows bushy gray. He's bald and proud of it. Entering Pappy's store, you feel like the happiest kid in the world.

You check your pocket or pack. The fifteen dollars is still there. Phe-ew! You take out the folded piece of paper on which (with your mom and dad's help) you've written the supplies you need to open your lemonade stand.

50 lemons
5 pounds of sugar
2 gallons of water

The water you can get for free from your kitchen. The lemons and sugar you have to buy at Pappy's store.

Lemons sell for twenty cents apiece. Sugar sells at forty cents per pound.

You're pretty good at math, so go ahead and add up the cost of the goods you need to make lemonade:

50 lemons at 20¢ each = $ _____

5 pounds of sugar at 40¢ per pound= $ _____

2 gallons of water free

_____

Total Purchases = $ _____

Having paid Pappy (who wishes you the best of luck with your new business), you load your supplies in your pack for the return trip. At home, you unload your supplies in the kitchen. Then, before you forget, you do a new scorecard that reflects the money spent buying goods to make your product. Since you spent twelve dollars on supplies, you need to take that amount out of Cash and record it somewhere new under Assets, since you're now the proud owner of fifty lemons and five pounds of sugar.

What do business people call the raw materials used in producing a product? Here's a hint. The word starts with "I" and ends with "Y." Need another hint? The inside letters are "N-V-E-N-T-O-R."

Did you guess "Inventory"? If so, you're absolutely right!

Inventory is a term for the raw materials, goods in process, and finished goods that a business plans to sell. Since you will use the lemons and sugar in your business, they are considered assets. So, Inventory is an Asset.

Take a moment and fill in the scorecard.

ASSETS		LIABILITIES	
CASH		NOTES PAYABLE	
		OWNER'S EQUITY	
INVENTORY		ORIGINAL INVESTMENT	
TOTAL ASSETS		TOTAL LIABILITIES & OWNER'S EQUITY	

Take at look at the last scorecard. Your cash is down, but it's been converted into inventory. In other words, you exchanged one asset for another.

Did this exchange change your total Assets? No. Your total Assets remain at fifteen dollars.

Was the right side of the scorecard affected by your trip to the store? No. The total Liabilities and Owner's Equity remains at fifteen dollars.

Does the left side equal the right side? Yes!

So, you're in balance!

It's time to make the lemonade.

Being careful not to waste a drop of lemon juice or a speck of sugar, being careful not to spill after you add the water, you discover that fifty lemons plus five pounds of sugar plus two gallons of water make enough lemonade to fill sixty glasses.

Let's put this into an equation, to determine what your COST OF PRODUCTION is.

50 lemons @ 20¢ each	$_____
5 lbs. Sugar @ 40¢/lb.	$_____
+ 2 gal. Water,	No Charge
60 Glasses=	$ _____

Now that we know your total Cost Of Production, let's figure out the cost per glass, or UNIT COST:

$$\frac{\text{COST of Production } \$\_\_\_\_}{^{\#}\text{ of glasses }\_\_\_\_} = \text{Cost per Unit (Glass) } \$\_\_\_\_\_$$

Hopefully, you came out with a Unit Cost of twenty cents. (Divide $12.00 by 60 glasses.)

You now know that it costs you twenty cents to produce one glass of lemonade.

Not just a glass of ordinary lemonade, but, in your humble opinion, the world's best glass of lemonade.

Then you ask yourself, "What will people pay for a glass of the world's best lemonade?" You certainly need to charge more than it cost you, otherwise you won't stay in business for long. But how much more?

You ask around. You ask your family and your friends and your neighbors and your dog or pet turtle. You think about what restaurants charge for drinks. You remember that last summer the kid down the street (who you don't like) got a dollar for his lemonade which was made from some awful-tasting powder mix. Not surprisingly (and to your secret delight), he only made a few dollars, and only because his parents felt sorry for him and bought a few glasses which they barely choked down.

Your product is excellent. Still, you don't want to charge so much as to scare away business. So, after concluding your research and pondering this important matter for a second or two, you decide to charge fifty cents a glass.

Finally, the big day arrives. The day your lemonade stand opens for business.

It's a warm, sunny, glorious day, full of promise, and there's, like, hundreds of people out walking their dogs and riding bikes and doing chores. Best of all, they all look incredibly thirsty!

In just a couple of hours, your cigar box starts to fill with quarters, dimes, nickels, pennies—and dollars! You can barely keep up with the demand. Your arm is about to fall off from pouring so many glasses of icy, cold, delicious, fresh, totally natural and organic lemonade, but you don't care because business is so good!

By the time you close up for the day, you've sold fifty—as in 5-0—glasses of lemonade! You add up all of the coins and dollars.

You sold twenty-five dollars of lemonade, on only your first day! Life doesn't get much better than this.

Then you remember that you had to spend money to make the lemonade. It cost 20¢ per glass, so it cost $10 to make 50 glasses. Now you figure if it cost $10 and you sold it for $25, you have $15 above and beyond your costs. Do you know what that's called? Profit or Earnings, right. In order to figure out your earnings, you need to subtract the COST OF GOODS SOLD (what it cost to make the fifty glasses of lemonade you sold) from your SALES (the money brought in by selling lemonade). The result of this subtraction is what business people call GROSS PROFIT.

Sales	$_____
Cost of Goods Sold (50 glasses @ 20¢ each)	$_____
Gross Profit (Earnings so far)	$_____

Let's reflect the day's business on a scorecard.

Remember, you sold fifty glasses of lemonade, which cost you ten dollars in Inventory to produce. Thus, the amount in Inventory was substantially reduced.

In return, though, in came twenty-five dollars of Cash, representing the sales of fifty glasses. Go ahead and record these changes.

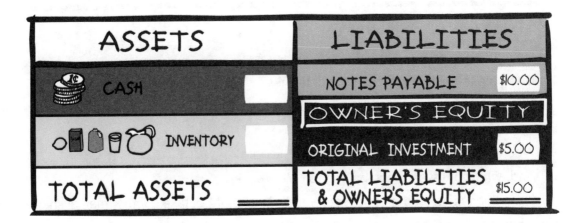

Does the left side equal the right side? No.

How much more do you have on the left side than the right side? Fifteen dollars.

Who owns that fifteen dollars? You do.

So we add $15 to Owner's Equity. But the earned $15 was not part of the Original Investment. So, what do you think we need to do? Yes, add another category to

Owner's Equity. We earned that $15, so we're going to add EARNINGS WEEK TO DATE to the Owner's Equity section.

Reflect your Earnings Week To Date on the right side of the next scorecard. Then add up the new total Liabilities and Owner's Equity.

Now, how much is on the left side? Thirty dollars.

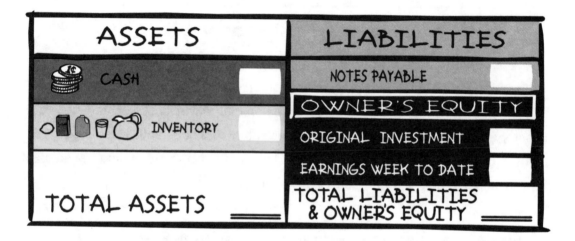

How much is on the right side? Thirty dollars.

Does the left side equal the right side? Yes.

What basic rule of accounting does this represent? Assets = Liabilities + Owner's Equity.

When did you earn that fifteen dollars? Just now.

And, who do the earnings belong to? Me, me, me!

Have things changed on your scorecard? And how! So, take another mental snapshot, one that records your first day running a lemonade stand—and making a profit!

That evening, as you practically have the money you made already spent in your mind, Mom and Dad drop a bombshell.

Those glasses you used at your lemonade stand, the ones you handled so carefully and afterwards washed 'til they sparkled and returned to the cupboard without as much as a scratch or chip on them—the glasses you *borrowed* from the kitchen—guess what.

Mom and Dad want to give you a lesson about running a business, and, without warning, decide to charge you a GLASS RENTAL FEE of two dollars!! Talk about tough love! You keep your mouth shut, but secretly you're convinced that Mom or Dad saw you making a profit and now want a piece of the action!

Worse yet, the next day, your best friend (or the kid you thought was your best friend) announces that he or she wants to be paid one dollar for a sign he or she painted for the lemonade stand.

Well, you decide, two can play this game! That afternoon, you decide you want to move the stand off your front yard, to the neighbors at the corner, which is sure to attract more business. Only problem is, the neighbors have been none too happy with you ever since they paid you to water their lawn while they were on vacation and you left the water on for about, oh, five hours too long and flooded their basement. But, hey, that was last summer, when you were just some silly kid. Now you're a budding businessperson running your own enterprise.

Nervous as a cat in a dog kennel, you knock on the neighbors' door. You explain your situation. To your relief, nobody mentions the flooded basement. They're impressed with your initiative, and suggest a fair price for the use of their front yard.

Now that you're a real business person, with real sales and expenses, you pay the neighbors two dollars to rent a spot on their lawn.

Two dollars for glass rental. A dollar for advertising. Another two dollars to rent the location.

Stop and figure out your EXPENSES.

Glass Rental	$_____
Advertising	$_____
Rent	$_____
Total Expenses =	$_____

Expenses are the costs of doing business other than those related to producing your product. You have to pay these expenses, regardless of how much or how little lemonade you make or sell. Things like glass rental, advertising, rent, and other things not directly related to the cost of making your product are in this category.

You pay your expenses out of Cash. Record the change on the next scorecard.

ASSETS			LIABILITIES	
CASH			NOTES PAYABLE	$10.00
			OWNER'S EQUITY	
INVENTORY			ORIGINAL INVESTMENT	$ 5.00
			EARNINGS WEEK TO DATE	$15.00
TOTAL ASSETS			TOTAL LIABILITIES & OWNER'S EQUITY	$30.00

Does the left side equal the right side? No.

In order to make both sides equal, you need to take five dollars off the right side. How about taking it out of the ten dollars you owe in Notes Payable? On second thought, the way Mom and Dad are acting, you might have to pay a finance charge for the original loan if you even broach the possibility!

What will the expenses reduce? Expenses reduce earnings.

So, you need to reduce your Earnings Week to Date by the amount you've incurred as Expenses in that period. Do so on the next score card.

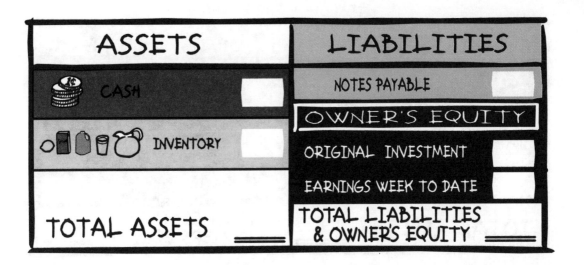

Now, does the left side equal the right? *Yes!*

Your cash is dropping but you still have enough left to pay off the ten-dollar IOU owed to Mom and Dad. You decide to do it, knowing your lemonade business will soon be challenging the likes of Nike, Disney, and Coca-Cola; even Microsoft!

You find the least wrinkled dollar bills and count out ten of them. Then you put them inside a card, which reads:

Thanks for the loan! I love you!

The card, in turn, goes into an envelope, which you seal and present to Mom and Dad.

They open the envelope, read the card and pocket the ten bucks with a big smile. "You did good. We're so proud of you!" They both give you a big hug. It's a proud, proud day! They give you back the IOU, which you tear up. Life doesn't get much better than this!

To pay off the IOU, you took ten dollars from Cash. But it allows you to reduce to zero the amount owed to Notes Payable. Record this transaction on the next scorecard.

ASSETS		LIABILITIES	
CASH		NOTES PAYABLE	
		OWNER'S EQUITY	
INVENTORY		ORIGINAL INVESTMENT	
		EARNINGS WEEK TO DATE	
TOTAL ASSETS		**TOTAL LIABILITIES & OWNER'S EQUITY**	

Does the left side equal the right side? It does.

So, what kind of scorecard is this? A Balance Sheet.

And what does a balance sheet always have to do? Balance.

Let's look at the purpose of a balance sheet.

The left side is Assets. Assets as a word isn't very kid-friendly. So, think of assets as THINGS AND STUFF.

The right side is Liabilities and Owner's Equity. Some more not very kid-friendly words. Liabilities represents the people you owe money to. And Owner's Equity is what you, as the owner of the business, own. Who owns things? Well, people, of course. So, think of the right side as PEOPLE.

Thus, the purpose of the Balance Sheet is to connect things to people. It shows you the things you have in your business. Then it connects the things you have to the people who own or have a claim on those things.

Now, go back and count how many Balance Sheets you filled out during this first week of your lemonade business. A lot! Because you filled one out for each transaction.

Would you normally fill out a Balance Sheet every single time you have a transaction? No.

How often a Balance Sheet is filled out varies from business to business. Banks, since they handle a great deal of money, do it on a daily basis. Some other businesses do it weekly, monthly, quarterly, and yearly. (A year is considered the basic accounting cycle.)

Since you plan to continue selling lemonade through the summer, we will use a week as our accounting period and do balance sheets with each activity.

Boy, you're doing great! But does a Balance Sheet tell you everything that happens in a business? Look back at your last Balance Sheet.

What happened this week at your lemonade stand that isn't recorded on the Balance Sheet?

Does the Balance Sheet show you what your sales were for the week? No. Does it tell you what the Cost of Goods Sold is? Nope.

Did you buy some inventory this week? Yes. Remember the trip to the store for supplies?

Did you sell some of your product? Sure did!

Does the balance sheet tell you how much Inventory you bought and sold? No.

Does it tell you how much you paid for all your Expenses (like the glass rental, advertising, and rent for using the neighbors' lawn)? No way!

Does it tell you how you made your Earnings? No. NO! And enough already with these questions!

Would a business want to know all of these things? You bet! The problem is, you can't find them by looking at a balance sheet. What will we need to do?

Create another scorecard.

We learned that a Balance Sheet shows us a moment in time, like a snapshot, but we need for our second scorecard to give us a record of events happening over a period of time. Events like buying inventory, making your product, selling it, and incurring expenses are happening over time.

What type of camera records a period of time? Something in the act of happening? A movie or video camera, of course.

So, we need a financial scorecard that acts like a motion picture. It will cover a period of time and shows motion. It has a beginning and end, just like a movie or video.

Luckily, this second type of scorecard exists, and it goes by a number of names. Do any on this list sound familiar?

Operating Statement.

Income Statement.

Profit & Loss (or P & L) Statement.

All of these terms represent the same type of financial statement. But, for our purposes, let's go with Income Statement.

If you need a break—maybe all of this talk about lemonade has made you incredibly thirsty—now's a good time. If you do take a break longer than a few minutes, you may want to review this section before moving ahead.

If, on the other hand, you have the stamina of a camel, next we're going to take up the Income Statement.

CHAPTER 2

○ ○ ○

Imagine how the first people to see motion pictures must have felt. Before the invention of the movies, the only way to capture the world was static—a frozen image, like a photograph or a painting. Then, with the first motion pictures, people were able to see the world as it really is! Always moving and changing. With things happening simultaneously at different places.

At the end of the last chapter, we said that if the Balance Sheet is like a snapshot of a business, then the Income Statement is like a movie. Does a photograph have a beginning and an end? (No, unless you wish to enlist some strange philosophical argument that will bore even your best friend.) Now, does a movie have a beginning and an end? (You get two chances to answer, and the first one doesn't count!)

Thus, an Income Statement has a beginning and an end.

Now, since we're talking about a financial scorecard and not some zillion-dollar Hollywood extravaganza, what exactly does an income statement show us?

It's called an income statement, so let's start by asking how income is generated in our lemonade business? From…what?

Did you say, "Sales"? Very good!

So, we begin with sales. Did it cost us any product to generate those sales? Yes. We need to find a name for what it costs us for goods sold.

Hmmmm. Any ideas out there?

Well, I'm going out on a limb now, but, with your permission, may I be bold enough to suggest Cost of Goods Sold?

Now, what does Cost of Goods Sold mean? The important thing is this: Cost of Goods Sold relates only to what? Our product or our lemonade.

Okay, let's do some figuring. If we subtract out the Cost of Goods Sold, not all the other stuff we spent money on, from Sales, what do we get? Gross Profit.

Gross Profit is sales minus cost of goods sold. (Net Profit is something different, which we'll get to shortly.)

$$\begin{array}{l} \text{Sales} \\ \underline{-\text{COGS (Cost of Goods Sold)}} \\ = \text{Gross Profit} \end{array}$$

Why do we call it gross profit? The word "gross" in German means "big" or "fat," so why is this the "fat profit"?

Because we haven't taken out all the other costs of doing business.

And what are examples of some of the other costs of doing business?

Did I hear someone say, "Expenses"? If so, you're right!

Just to have our lemonade stand open out on the sidewalk did we have certain expenses? Yes! We had glass rental and rent to the neighbors for our location and some advertising. So, are Expenses the cost of being in business, regardless whether or not we sell a single glass of lemonade? 'Fraid so!

A moment ago, we said the lemonade or the Cost of Goods Sold is subtracted from our Sales and then we've got our Gross Profit. Now, let's subtract out all the other Expenses and we get what? (Now, those of us curious about Net Profit, chime in!)

Sales

-COGS

= Gross Profit

-Expenses

= Net Profit

Notice how Net Profit is at the bottom line of this formula? So, it stands to reason that Net Profit is often called the...?

Bottom line.

You can see that our Income Statement separates costs into two categories—Cost of Goods Sold for all the costs of producing our product, and Expenses for all the non-production costs of running the business. For a business that does not have a tangible product (i.e., a service business) the two categories are Cost of Sales or Cost of Services and Expenses.

Now, go back to Chapter One and put in the numbers for the formula below, so we can see where we stand with the bottom line.

Sales	$_____
-COGS	$_____
Gross Profit	$_____
-Expenses	$_____
Net Profit	$_____

Let's take a moment and review.

The purpose of the Income Statement is to keep track of sales minus Cost of Goods Sold, which gives us Gross Profit. Then, we subtract all the other Expenses, which gives us our what?

Net Profit.

What is another name for net profit?

Net Income or the bottom line.

So—earnings, net profit, net income and the bottom line—are they all the same?

Absolutely!

Okay, let's get back to business! We're going to go through a detailed Income Statement line by line. You may want to get a straight edge (a ruler; even an envelope or a piece of paper will do), to help you keep things clean and simple.

INCOME STATEMENT

```
INCOME STATEMENT          Begin: Monday A.M. End: Sunday P.M.
SALES                                                    $ _____

        Beginning Inventory              $ _____
        + Purchases
            Sugar                          _____
            Lemons                         _____
        Total Available for Sale                  $ _____
        - Ending Inventory                          _____
    = COST OF GOODS SOLD                                     _____
    GROSS PROFIT =                                           _____
    EXPENSES
        •                                  _____
        •                                  _____
        •                                  _____

    = TOTAL EXPENSES                                         _____
    NET PROFIT                                      $ _____
```

We said that an Income Statement was like a motion picture in that it has a beginning and an end. This length of time can be a week, a month, a quarter of a year, etc. Whatever the length, it's called the ACCOUNTING PERIOD.

Remember when you were a kid and how it was hard to look beyond the next day or two, much less well into the next week or month? Remember how agonizing it was to wake up early and have to wait and wait and wait and wait until your afternoon party guests started to arrive? So, since we're running a lemonade stand, let's not make our accounting period too long. Say, a week.

So, let's begin on Monday and end on Sunday. Wow, we've been in business one whole week! That's longer than a lot of good ideas last.

Do you remember what our total sales were for the week?

If not, check back in Chapter One.

Hopefully, you came up with twenty-five dollars in total Sales. Put it all the way to the right on the Income Statement. Why? Because it's a total figure, and we're going to do something with it in a little while.

By the way, you probably notice that it's pretty awkward to have to go back to look up all the information. Do you know how a business organizes the information so it is found easily? Businesses create what's called a GENERAL LEDGER, which is a moment by moment record of every thing that happens. In the good old days of business, every entry in the General Ledger was recorded by hand. (Remember Scrooge poring over his ledger in *A Christmas Carol*?) Today, almost all businesses use a computer. The software is programmed to create categories for each item and sums them for the financial statements.

Let's drop down to the next line. What's it say? Beginning Inventory.

Did we have any inventory before we started this week? No. We didn't even have a business before this week!

So reason dictates that the amount of the Beginning Inventory is what? Zero. Go ahead and write it in.

Then, to start the business, you went and bought what? Sugar for $2.00 and Lemons for $10.00. Write that in.

Drop down to the next line.

Given all this, how much available for sale did you have during the week? (Beginning Inventory + Purchases.) But did you sell it all? No.

Drop down to the next line.

What do we subtract out? The lemonade not sold. What's it called? Ending Inventory.

Okay, since we didn't sell it, we can't count it as a part of the Cost of Goods that we actually sold. Right? Right.

Drop down to the next line.

Math time. Take Beginning Inventory + Purchases - Ending Inventory. The result is the actual Cost of Goods Sold. Which is...? (Write your answer on the Income Statement.)

Write in the COGS. While you are doing it, notice that this figure is also where? On the right.

Which means we're going to do what with it?

Subtract it.

Now, subtract the Cost of Goods Sold from our Sales—and what do you have? (Write it in the next line, way to the right).

What do we call this amount. It's our Gross Profit!

Now, what do have to subtract next? *Expenses.*

Our Expenses include…what? *Well, there was Glass Rental and Advertising, and Rent. Go back to Chapter One for the actual costs, then write them on your Income Statement*

What are your total Expenses? *Add up the Expenses.*

Notice that this total figure goes where…? *All the way over on the right.*

Which means we're going to…? *Subtract it.*

Subtract it from what? *The Gross Profit.*

Which leave us with…? *Our Net Profit*

In what amount? (Write it down on the Income Statement.)

Take a moment and wipe your brow and rest your racing pulse.

Now compare the numbers on the Income Statement to the numbers on your last balance sheet that is on page 18. Do you see any numbers that are the same on the Balance Sheet and Income statement? *Earnings and Net Profit.*

So, are these two figures the same—Earnings week to date (on the balance sheet) and Net Profit (on the income statement)? *Yes!*

A while back we compared financial scorecards to snapshots and motion pictures. Let's try looking at them in another way.

A Balance Sheet is like the map of the state you live in. What do you see on a state map? (Cities, main roads, rivers, mountains, etc.) Basically, a pretty big picture short on details.

Let's focus on one item on the Balance Sheet—Earnings. Pretend it's like the city or town you live in. The state map shows you where it is, but does not give you any details. What kind of map do you need to see the streets, the streams, the local landmarks? (A city or town map.) It's like a blow up and that's what the Income Statement is. It's a blow up or detailed "city map" of how we got to our Earnings. The Balance Sheet just says you had $10 in Earnings. The Income Statement shows that you had $25 in Sales, $10 in COGS, and $5 in Expenses.

Returning to the world of accounting, we take earnings week to date on the Balance Sheet and blow it up and what do we get?

The Income Statement!

Let's look at the numbers on your last Balance Sheet in Chapter One and the Income Statement we just filled out on page 25.

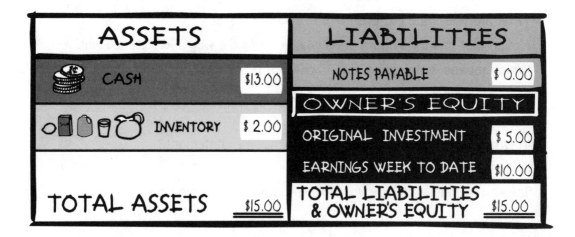

ASSETS		LIABILITIES	
CASH	$13.00	NOTES PAYABLE	$0.00
		OWNER'S EQUITY	
INVENTORY	$2.00	ORIGINAL INVESTMENT	$5.00
		EARNINGS WEEK TO DATE	$10.00
TOTAL ASSETS	$15.00	**TOTAL LIABILITIES & OWNER'S EQUITY**	$15.00

INCOME STATEMENT	Begin: Monday A.M. End: Sunday P.M.		
SALES			$ 25.00
Beginning Inventory	$ 0.00		
+ Purchases			
Sugar	2.00		
Lemons	10.00		
Total Available for Sale		$ 12.00	
- Ending Inventory		2.00	
= COST OF GOODS SOLD			10.00
GROSS PROFIT =			15.00
EXPENSES			
• Glass Rental		2.00	
• Advertising		1.00	
• Rent		2.00	
			5.00
= TOTAL EXPENSES			
NET PROFIT			$ 10.00

Where, again, are the two financial statements related? Net Profit and Earnings.

Any other number the same? YES! Inventory

Why do you think our Ending Inventory is on the Balance Sheet and the Income Statement? Because we haven't used it!

We can't take it as part of our Cost of Goods Sold because we haven't sold it. So, we subtract it from our total available for sale. And on the Balance Sheet, since we haven't sold it, does it have value? Yes!

Is it something we can sell at another time? Yes! So, we leave it here in Ending Inventory.

So this is the end of the week, and what kind of Balance Sheet is this? An Ending Balance Sheet.

And, if this is an Ending Balance Sheet, what kind of inventory is this? Ending Inventory.

Let's just look at these two financial statements and how they're linked together. We started with what kind of Balance Sheet on Monday? A Beginning Balance Sheet.

And we ended on Sunday night with our what? Ending Balance Sheet. They give us two snapshots in time. Now, the truth is, we actually completed a bunch of Balance Sheets—one for each transaction. We will keep doing that throughout this book, but companies just generate a Beginning and Ending Balance Sheet at the start and end of their accounting period.

So, at the start of this week, our beginning inventory was what? ZERO. And ending Inventory is what? Two Dollars.

Our beginning Earnings are what? Zero. And our ending Earnings are what? Ten Dollars.

The thing that connects the beginning and ending balance sheets is what? The movie or the Income Statement.

It's like this. The Beginning Balance Sheet shows us where we started, the Ending Balance Sheet shows us where we are, and what shows us how we got there? The Income Statement.

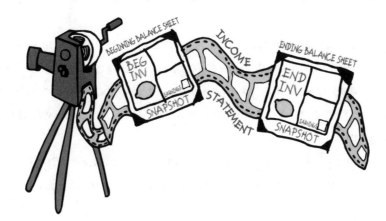

You're doing great! Both as an entrepreneur and in understanding the basics of accounting.

Since you're doing so great, here's a little challenge. One item that occurred this week does not show up on our final Balance Sheet or on the Income Statement.

Here are three questions for you:

What item is it?

Why is it not on either statement?

What does the absence of this item tell us about our record keeping so far?

The answer to question one is, the loan payback to Mom and Dad. Why is that not on the Balance Sheet? Because it's paid back. A loan only shows up on the Balance Sheet when you still owe it.

To understand why it's not on the Income Statement you have to ask yourself how you got the money. Did you earn it? *No. Your parents loaned it to you.* Did it really cost you anything to pay it back? *Not really, you just gave them back their money after using it for a while.* So the principal of a loan, the actual amount borrowed, does not go on an Income Statement because you didn't "earn it." What would have affected Earnings? *Interest. Interest on the loan which would have shown up as an expense. Thank goodness Mom and Dad didn't think of that!*

Getting to question three—what does this tell us about our records? *They are incomplete.*

Guess what, two financial statements do not present the whole picture! You need at least three statements. And what is the third one? (You probably already know, but just in case, what was affected both when you got and paid the loan? *Of course, CASH FLOW.* So, the third statement keeps track of Cash Flow. We will develop it in detail in a later chapter.)

Phew! It's the end of the week. Want to work on Sunday? What? And miss a great day to relax, to hit the local swimming hole or pal around with friends? Let's take Sunday off.

What are we going to do with those ten glasses of left over Inventory? Put it in the refrigerator and put a sign on it that says:

For commercial use only!
Do not touch upon penalty of death!

Time for a break.

Before you leave, give yourselves a gold star for doing such a good job your first week in the business. Good Job!

CHAPTER 3

It's Monday. A sunny morning, with the promise of getting really hot by noon. Which can mean but one thing to you, the budding beverage billionaire. It's a great day to be selling lemonade!

Last week wasn't bad, for a beginner. But from now on, well, look out world!

First, let's take a look at our last Balance Sheet.

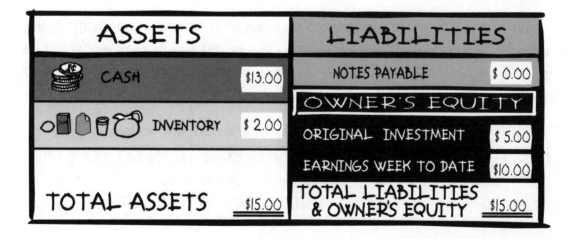

ASSETS			LIABILITIES	
CASH	$13.00		NOTES PAYABLE	$ 0.00
			OWNER'S EQUITY	
INVENTORY	$ 2.00		ORIGINAL INVESTMENT	$ 5.00
			EARNINGS WEEK TO DATE	$10.00
TOTAL ASSETS	$15.00		TOTAL LIABILITIES & OWNER'S EQUITY	$15.00

Now, this Balance Sheet is for which week? Last week.

Therefore, it's what kind of Balance Sheet? Ending Balance Sheet.

So, this is last week's Ending Balance Sheet, and where is our ending Inventory? In the refrigerator.

And now it's Monday morning and you go and open up the refrigerator and what's in there? Your lemonade, or someone has some serious answering to do!

Let's say, for the sake of household peace, that, sure enough, your lemonade is still in the fridge. This Ending Inventory from last week becomes what kind of Inventory for this week? Beginning Inventory, right!

One last time: the ending Inventory automatically becomes what kind of Inventory? Right! The Beginning Inventory for the next week.

The Ending Balance Sheet is for last week, so we need to make what kind of Balance Sheet for the beginning of week number 2? Beginning Balance Sheet.

There's one more thing we need to do to convert last week's Ending Balance Sheet to this week's Beginning Balance Sheet. Do you know what that is? The earnings.

The earnings we have were good for which week?

Last week, the first week of our business. As a result, these earnings are now what? History.

What are earnings that are history, or earnings from past accounting periods called? Retained Earnings.

Yes, Retained Earnings, and we need to make room for our earnings for when? This week.

We're going to take these earnings from last week and roll them up into a new category called Retained Earnings, making room for this week's earnings. We will do this to a sing-along so everyone sing to the tune of "Roll Out The Barrels." Ready? A one, and a two...

Roll up the earnings, lemons are turning to gold.

Roll up the earnings, lemons are turning to gold.

You've got your earnings rolled up. Now, you should have $10 in Retained Earnings and zero in Earnings Week to Date. Complete the Balance Sheet below, to reflect this.

ASSETS		LIABILITIES	
CASH		NOTES PAYABLE	
		TOTAL LIABILITIES	
INVENTORY		OWNER'S EQUITY	
		ORIGINAL INVESTMENT	
		RETAINED EARNINGS	
		EARNINGS WEEK TO DATE	
		TOTAL OWNER'S EQUITY	
TOTAL ASSETS		TOTAL LIABILITIES & OWNER'S EQUITY	

Retained Earnings will show us all the earnings in a business from when? From prior accounting periods.

What exactly are Retained Earnings? We said they are earnings from past accounting periods. There are only two things that happen to earnings—you either retain them in the business or distribute them to the owners of the company. In a corporation, a distribution of earnings means the company pays a dividend to the stockholders. Earnings that have not been distributed are retained in the company.

For this week, our earnings will be recorded in Earnings Week to Date—because we always work in the current period.

Let's review. At the beginning of each new week in order to update our Ending Balance Sheet to make it a Beginning Balance Sheet we're going to do what?

Roll up the earnings and retain them in the company and convert Ending Inventory to Beginning Inventory.

Great! Now we're ready to start the new week.

As you wake Monday morning, you think, Why stay small? There's no time like the present to start growing my lemonade business.

Real businesspeople don't go on borrowing money from Mom and Dad. Real businesspeople borrow money from a real bank.

After breakfast, you put on clean clothes and brush your hair. Then you get Mom or Dad to drive you to your neighborhood bank. You show the banker your financial statements.

The banker is dressed in a really nice suit that is incapable of attracting even a speck of dust. Meanwhile, while clean, you're dressed in sneakers, jeans, and a T-shirt that says KIDS RULE!! As you sit in a chair that's too big, you have to remind yourself to stop kicking your legs and to sit up straight and look grownup.

"I'll be a good customer, I promise," you tell the banker in a squeaky voice. "You won't have to worry about getting your money back. I borrowed ten dollars from my parents and already paid it back."

The banker looks up and nods.

"Look at my balance sheet," you say proudly. "I have $13.00 in cash. I have some inventory, no debt, and I started my business with five bucks and I had earnings last week of ten dollars."

The banker glances over your scorecard, and nods. "Impressive," the banker says. "There are a lot of grownup businesspeople who don't keep this good a record."

You're pretty sure the banker just complimented you, though it's hard to tell because the banker's eyebrows and lips hardly move. "Do you give loans to kids?" you ask.

"We don't discriminate because of a potential customer's age, gender, religious, racial, or ethnic identity," the banker says.

Which you're pretty sure means "Yes" to your question.

"Look at my income statement," you go on. "Last week I had sales of $25. My gross profit was $15, these are my expenses, with a net profit of $10. Would you loan me $50.00?"

Impressed, the bank loans you $50.00 cash.

"Hey, thanks," you tell the banker. "I appreciate your interest in my business. You won't be sorry! Come by my stand on your way home." You start to leave, but you can't help but turn back and say, "You know, with an original investment of $5 and a net profit of $10, that's a 200 percent return on my investment. Hey, how's the bank doing?"

Smiling, the banker wishes you well.

Now, please demonstrate what just happened on the next scorecard.

First, what comes in? *Cash.*

So bring in $50.

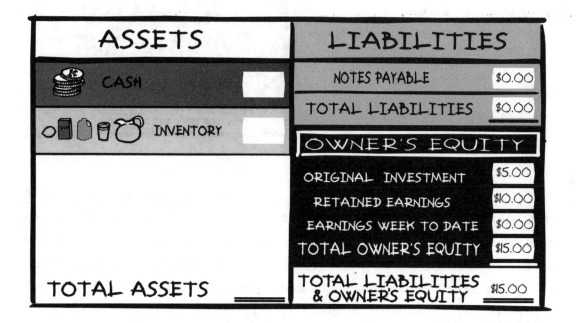

Are we in balance? *No.*

Who do we owe now? *The banker for $50.00*

Where do we show it? *Notes payable.*

Demonstrate this on the next scorecard.

ASSETS		LIABILITIES	
CASH		NOTES PAYABLE	
		TOTAL LIABILITIES	
INVENTORY	$2.00	OWNER'S EQUITY	
		ORIGINAL INVESTMENT	$5.00
		RETAINED EARNINGS	$10.00
		EARNINGS WEEK TO DATE	$0.00
		TOTAL OWNER'S EQUITY	
TOTAL ASSETS		TOTAL LIABILITIES & OWNER'S EQUITY	

Are we in balance now? *Yes!*

By the time you get home from the bank, it's already lunch. It looks like it might rain. So you decide to give yourself the rest of the day off. (It helps when you're your own boss!) But you're afraid that the lemonade in the fridge might not last until tomorrow. You decide to sell your remaining inventory for $2.00 to your best friend at cost, for cash. Your best friend is always thirsty and loves your lemonade, so it's a win-win. The only downer to an otherwise glorious day is that, since you're home, your mom and dad insist you clean up your room.

Show the financial results of what just happened. How? By reducing inventory? *Yes, the whole thing.* But if you reduce inventory to zero, where do the two dollars go? *Well, your friend gave you two dollars, so add them to your Cash.*

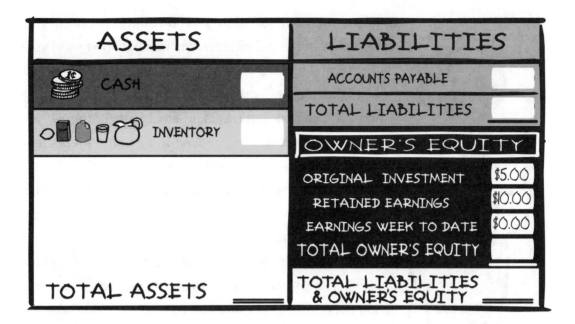

Are we in balance? Yes!

What happened? The two dollars' worth lemonade turned into what? Two dollars in Cash.

Did anything change in terms of total assets? No.

Did we have sale? Yes.

We just didn't make any what? Profit.

Will this transaction show up on our Income Statement? Yes. As part of what? Total Sales. Make a reminder to yourself to put this into your sales total when you fill out your Income Statement at the end of the week.

After you return from your very brief vacation (interrupted by having to clean your room), you need to make up some new lemonade. You overhear Mom and Dad talking about paying their account at the grocery store, where they have a charge account. Hey, you think, maybe I can set up an account. It's worth a try, right?

You tell your parents your idea and they say it's worth a try. So, you get your bike out of the garage and pedal like crazy (watching for cars and crazy dogs, of course) down to the grocery store.

Outside, you wait to catch your breath. You check your appearance in the big window. You moisten the tips of your finger with a little spit and plaster down the hair which got messed riding your bike. Your parents hate when you use spit, but this is an emergency! After all, you want Pappy Parker, the grocer, to see an entrepreneur, not just some sweaty kid.

"Hey, Pappy," you say, entering the store. "I'm in business now, just like you. It's tough competing against the really big companies, isn't it? Us little guys need to stick together. How about one businessperson helping out another? I'd like to buy 10 pounds of sugar at 40 cents/pound, for a total of $4.00."

"I can handle that," Pappy says with a wink. The grocer's store is a family business. It sells everything from great fresh produce to racks of snacks in one big room. Even though the place is crowded with stuff and the linoleum on the floor is, like, fifty years old, you like it better than the enormous, impersonal supermarket. One reason is that good ol' Pappy gives every kid who comes in a free cookie!

Another reason is the great customer service that the Pappy and everyone else working at his store provide. The grocery staff knows every customer by name. And you'll always remember the time Pappy wouldn't let your mom buy some fruit that looked too ripe. Instead, the ol' Pap left the register and selected the best piece of fruit on display, then gave it to your mom for free. Yes sir, that Pappy sure knows how treat his customers right!

You really like good ol' Pappy. He's like your favorite uncle—or grandpa. This gives you the courage to add, "And I'd like to purchase the sugar on credit."

"Credit? Tell me, please, why would I give you credit?"

"Well, you give my parents credit. Can I have credit too?"

"But your parents work for a living," Pappy points out.

"I'm working for a living, too," you reply. "I'm selling fresh lemonade."

"Lemonade? Is it good lemonade?" he asks.

"The absolute best, most totally awesome lemonade in this part of the galaxy," you say.

"That good? Are you trying to put me out of business?" Pappy says this with a smile.

"Just the opposite," you quickly respond. (It amazes you that every so often the ol' brain charges in with a great reply!) "After all, the more lemonade I sell, the more lemons and sugar I'll need to buy from you. Plus maybe paper cups and napkins. And maybe one day I'll add cookies, which I'll get from your bakery because they're the best around." You run out of great ideas and hope it's enough to win over Pappy.

He lives in the neighborhood and always gives free stuff to your school. Pappy's known you and your family for a long time.

"Well, it sounds like you figured it all out," he observes. "Maybe one day you'll help me out with my business?"

"You'll give me credit?" you ask hopefully.

"I'll give you $4.00 in credit," Pappy says, handing you a piece of paper to sign.

Home, you unpack the grocery sack. What financial category is packed inside? *Inventory.*

What kind of inventory? *Sugar.*

How much sugar? *$4.00.* **What color?** *White—just checking!*

Did you pay CASH for the sugar? *No! Is this a great country, or what?!*

Do we owe money? *Yes.*

In order for the grocer to keep track of the credit, what have we set up? *An account.*

And it's payable to whom? *The grocer.*

What do businesses call this sort of thing? *ACCOUNTS PAYABLE.*

So, now we have our second kind of liability. We had the note with the banker and now the account set up with the grocer. Demonstrate this latest transaction below.

ASSETS		LIABILITIES	
CASH		ACCOUNTS PAYABLE	
		NOTES PAYABLE	
INVENTORY		TOTAL LIABILITIES	
		OWNER'S EQUITY	
		ORIGINAL INVESTMENT	
		RETAINED EARNINGS	
		EARNINGS WEEK TO DATE	
		TOTAL OWNER'S EQUITY	
TOTAL ASSETS		TOTAL LIABILITIES & OWNER'S EQUITY	

What's the difference between the two kinds of liabilities?

The Notes Payable from the bank shows that the bank gave you what? Money! And the Accounts Payable with the grocer shows that the grocer gave you what? Sugar or Inventory.

So, is it fair to say that Notes Payable has to do with money owed to someone else for money received, and Accounts Payable has to do with some things we got for our business which we have to pay for someday? Yes. In other words, for Notes Payable we got cash and for Accounts Payable we got goods or services.

There is another difference between Notes Payable and Accounts Payable. It has to do with time. Generally speaking, a loan from a bank (Notes Payable) and a credit account (Accounts Payable) from a store have different payback periods. In other words, one is for a short time and one is for a longer time.

Which is which? Accounts Payable is short-term, usually due in full in maybe thirty days. Notes Payable is long-term, maybe several years. That's why Accounts Payable is the first item in Liabilities—they are generally ordered as they come due.

Any other difference? HINT: What's one thing all bank loans come with that store credits generally don't come with providing you promptly pay off your balance? *Interest!*

Which has interest? *Notes Payable. Usually, Accounts Payable does not have interest unless you don't pay on time.*

In both cases, we're establishing what? *Credit!* Hey, we're pretty sharp entrepreneurs! Or at least a lot like Mom and Dad and most other businesses and consumers! We owe people money! Talk about feeling grownup!

Now that we have some credit, it's time to buy some other supplies. You buy 100 lemons at 20 cents/lemon. You want to keep in good with the grocer so you pay in cash.

The amount goes out of Cash, and into...what? *Inventory.*

How much inventory? *Twenty dollars in lemons come in.*

Again, what did we do? We exchanged $20.00 in cash for what? *Twenty dollars in inventory.*

Did we, in fact, exchange one asset for another. *Yes.*

Bring the next scorecard up to date, reflecting these transactions.

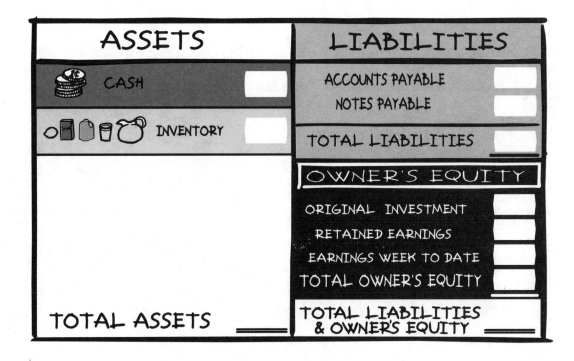

Are we in balance? Yes.

You should have $69 in Assets, $54 in Liabilities, and $15 in Equity; the sum of the right side total is $69.

You're doing great. You're especially patient with all this record-keeping stuff. But, believe me, you'll be glad later.

Now that our financial record-keeping is up to date, it's time to take a break (if you wish). Then, let's make up a fresh batch of the world's greatest lemonade!

CHAPTER 4

Now that you're a pro at mixing lemonade, you make up a good sized batch. The batch takes fifty lemons (@ 20¢/each) and five pounds of sugar (@ 40¢/lb.), to make sixty glasses. What's the cost of production?

Before we answer, let's add another element. So far, you have made all your own lemonade, but this morning you decided to take off some time to go biking with friends. Still, you want to have the lemonade stand opened as soon as you return.

So, you ask your older sister if she'll make the lemonade for you. Most of the time you and your sister are pretty good buddies. But, suddenly, with your friends waiting outside, she turns into Scrooge!

"Why should I do you any favors?" she asks.

"Come on," you plead. "Just this once. I promise I won't bug you the next time you're on the phone."

"That's not good enough," she replies. "I'm no dummy. I've heard all that cash rattling in the cigar box. You have to pay me if you want your lemonade ready."

Well, she has you now. Boy, wait until you're rich and famous! See her come crawling for a favor then! But that's a few years down the road, and now your friends are screaming for you to hurry up.

"You win," you say with a sigh. "How much do you want?"

She smiles. She never is very modest in victory. "I want one dollar to make 60 glasses."

First, you get angry at her smugness, then, you force yourself to calm down and decide to pay it. After all, business is business. "Fine," you agree.

You give her the buck and head out the door. Once on your bike, with your friends, you reason this out. A dollar in labor cost is too much for sixty glasses—and it will lower your profit. But you figure you can afford it just this once.

A while later, refreshed from your ride, you return in time for the afternoon sales and see, to your relief, that your sister has done her job well. There in the refrigerator are 60 glasses of fresh lemonade. Say, maybe this boss thing isn't so bad, after all!

Seriously, let's look at our Inventory. We've got two types of Inventory here. What do we call the lemons and sugar? *Raw materials.*

And what kind of inventory is lemonade? *Finished goods.*

Now, while we (or Big Sister) were making it, what kind of inventory was it? *Work-in-process—or WIP. Work-in-process is a big item for manufacturing companies.*

We go from raw materials to work-in-process to finished goods.

We didn't use up all of our raw materials, though, for this batch. As a result, we have both raw materials and finished goods in our inventory. Are the raw materials considered available for sale? *Yes.*

For record-keeping purposes, all Inventory is available for sale.

Before we greet our afternoon customers, let's fill out another Balance Sheet to reflect that we've just paid labor to make our product.

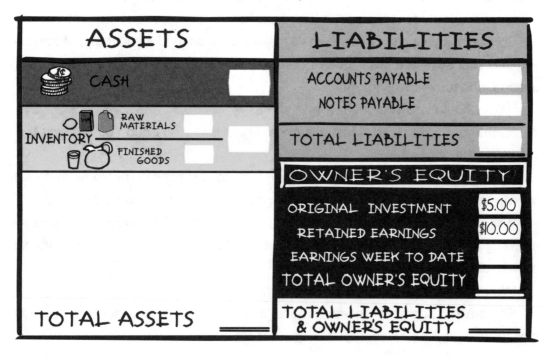

How did you account for the labor? It reduced Cash by $1.00.

Here, though, is where it gets a little tricky. Many people would say, let's expense it and reduce our earnings.

However, in this case, you cannot expense the dollar—and you may know why. It has to do with the job Big Sister was doing—specifically her labor was to produce your product. Literally, her labor increased the value of the Inventory—so, in truth, you should have taken the $1 from Cash and added $1 to Inventory. As a result, Cash is now $44 and Inventory is $25. Note that our Balance Sheet from now on will separate raw materials and finished goods. You should have $12 in raw materials and $13 in Finished Goods, and $25 in Total Inventory.

You can see now that the Cost of Production labor is "tied up" in inventory. That $1 cost cannot be recognized (or expensed) until the Inventory is sold. That's one reason companies closely manage inventory quantities and always want to sell it quickly.

So, let's get selling!

It's a hot day and you're sweating, but it's OK because sales are very, very good. Your new location pays off, and easily earns back what you spent renting it. Kids from other neighborhoods—total strangers!—come by on their bikes, having heard about your great lemonade.

Some friends come by, with their tongues practically dragging on the pavement. "Please, please, give us some lemonade!"

"Give?" you repeat.

"We left our money at home," they explain. "But we're good for it, we promise!"

Since they're friends, you let them buy their lemonade on credit.

By the end of the afternoon, your arm is about to fall off from pouring so much lemonade. But it's all worth it when you total up your sales.

60 glasses for 50 cents each
40 glasses cash and 20 glasses on account

What's your total sales? Thirty dollars. Twenty dollars Cash. Ten dollars on Account.

Let's review what happened here.

Did you sell all the lemonade you made up? *Yes.*

How many glasses did you sell? *Sixty.*

What goes out of the business? *Inventory.*

How much? *Thirteen dollars.*

What comes in? *Cash.*

Cash for how much? *Twenty dollars.*

So we get $20 for the forty glasses we sold for Cash. What else happened?

Some of your friends said they wanted to buy some lemonade, but they didn't have any money. Their parents hadn't given them what? *Their allowance.* So, they wanted to buy now, and pay when? *Later.* Did you, ever kind and wonderful and always on the outlook to increase sales, decide to sell to them? *Yes.* Admit it, did it make you a little nervous. *A bit. Sure.* Did you make a record of the sale? *Yes.*

Sure, the kids on credit are your friends and all—but this is business! You got out your little notebook and recorded these sales... Ted, 1 glass,.50, Natalie, 2 glasses, 1.00...etc.

What did your friends do? They set up an account with whom?

Right, with you!

Did those thirsty kids get the lemonade? *Sure did.*

Was it a sale? *Yes!*

You just didn't receive any...what? *Cash.*

So, you had to set up an account.

Is this money owed to you right now? *Yes!*

Pretty soon, though, you'll want to go out and receive what? *The green stuff. Cash.*

So, if you have to set up an account and plan to receive the cash from your friends, the account is called what? *Accounts Receivable.* Is an Account Receivable something we have? *Yes.*

That means it's a what? *An asset.* Since it's money we are going to get soon, is it almost cash? *Yes.* What color should we make it? *Almost green.*

Did your friends promise, promise, promise to pay you? *Yes. And even did a pinkie swear!* They said they were good for it. (And if you can't trust your friends, who can you?) But, honestly, have they paid you yet? *No, not yet, but they better!*

They said they were going to get their allowance at the end of the week? *Yes. Right before they chugged down the lemonade.*

Was this a good idea? Why do businesses let people set up accounts? Ever hear of "buy now, pay later"? Right, to generate more sales!

Bring the next scorecard up to date, to show the changes in assets.

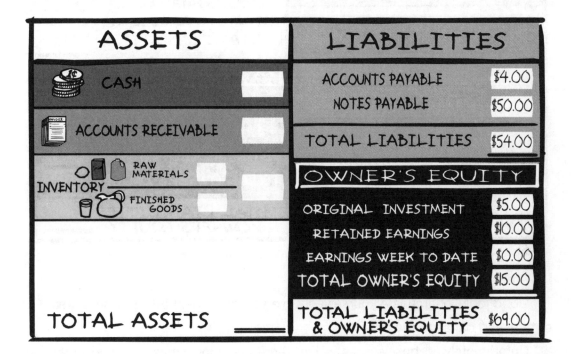

ASSETS		LIABILITIES	
CASH		ACCOUNTS PAYABLE	$4.00
		NOTES PAYABLE	$50.00
ACCOUNTS RECEIVABLE		TOTAL LIABILITIES	$54.00
INVENTORY — RAW MATERIALS		OWNER'S EQUITY	
FINISHED GOODS		ORIGINAL INVESTMENT	$5.00
		RETAINED EARNINGS	$10.00
		EARNINGS WEEK TO DATE	$0.00
		TOTAL OWNER'S EQUITY	$15.00
TOTAL ASSETS		TOTAL LIABILITIES & OWNER'S EQUITY	$69.00

So are we in balance? *No.*

What do we need to show?

We need to record our profit or earnings for the week.

So how much did we have in total sales? *$30.*

We had $20 in cash and $10 on account.

How much did it cost us in lemonade? *$13.00*

So if it cost us $13.00 and we sold it for $30.00, what's our profit or earnings for this sale? *$17.00*

Record your profit or earnings below.

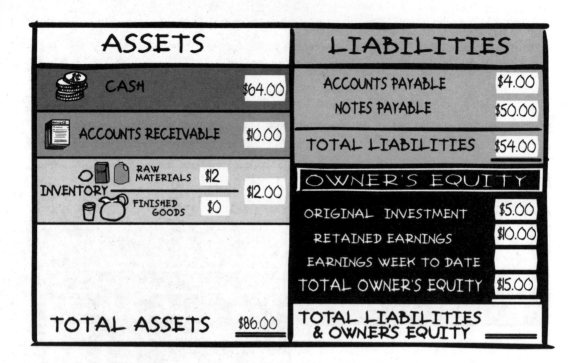

ASSETS		LIABILITIES	
CASH	$64.00	ACCOUNTS PAYABLE	$4.00
		NOTES PAYABLE	$50.00
ACCOUNTS RECEIVABLE	$10.00	TOTAL LIABILITIES	$54.00
INVENTORY RAW MATERIALS $12 FINISHED GOODS $0	$12.00	OWNER'S EQUITY	
		ORIGINAL INVESTMENT	$5.00
		RETAINED EARNINGS	$10.00
		EARNINGS WEEK TO DATE	
		TOTAL OWNER'S EQUITY	$15.00
TOTAL ASSETS	$86.00	TOTAL LIABILITIES & OWNER'S EQUITY	

Are we in balance? Yes.

Good job! Congratulate yourselves! Give yourself a high five! Put on a great CD or tape and dance to the music!

Unfortunately, in business as in life, there are good times and bad times. No sooner are you dancing around your room than the phone rings.

It's a friend of yours telling you that one of your other friends, Johnny, the incredibly thirsty one who bought eight glasses on account has—gasp!—moved away!

After throwing yourself to the ground and stamping the floor with your fists and crying for the first time since you were really hurt, you conclude that this moved-away, no-good friend is unlikely to pay his debt. Given this sobering realization, you also conclude that this act of treachery will have a negative impact on your business and your financial records. Are this eight glasses a loss? Of course! What do you call this kind of loss? Bad Debt. This Bad Debt expense = $4.00

Now what are we going to do?

Even as you regain control, you still can't believe it! That kid promised to pay you! He even gave a pinkie swear, which is like the highest oath a kid can take! You figured he was good for it. But now he's left town. Oh, well, at least he didn't leave town thirsty—thanks to you!

Do we have to recognize the loss? Yes. We had $10.00 in Accounts Receivable, four of which belonged to that totally rude and worthless weasel cheater and all-around bad kid who you were once foolish enough to trust and call your friend. He'll probably end up in prison, or politics—or both!

So what are we going to do? You list your options.

Send out the collection agency.

Hire a hitman.

Hire a lawyer.

Tell your parents.

Get your big brother or sister to beat him up.

Put a spell on him so he stays short his whole life.

E-mail the President to call out the National Guard.

But you're a business person, remember? So what do we do to recognize a bad debt?

Reduce Accounts Receivable? Sadly, yes.

Reduce it by how much? Four whole dollars.

Are we in balance now? No.

Is the Bad Debt a cost of doing business? Yes.

And a cost of doing business is called what? An expense.

And expenses always reduce what? Earnings.

So, reduce earnings by $4.00 to reflect the bad debt expense.

ASSETS			LIABILITIES	
CASH		$64.00	ACCOUNTS PAYABLE	$4.00
			NOTES PAYABLE	$50.00
ACCOUNTS RECEIVABLE			TOTAL LIABILITIES	$54.00
INVENTORY	RAW MATERIALS $12	$12.00	**OWNER'S EQUITY**	
	FINISHED GOODS $0		ORIGINAL INVESTMENT	$5.00
			RETAINED EARNINGS	$10.00
			EARNINGS WEEK TO DATE	
			TOTAL OWNER'S EQUITY	
TOTAL ASSETS		____	TOTAL LIABILITIES & OWNER'S EQUITY	____

Now, are we in balance? Yes.

On which financial statement are we going to record the Bad Debt expense? Right, we'd write it on the Income Statement. For how much? $4.00 (Expenses).

Take a moment and catch your breath.

Sobered by the experience of the bad debt, you decide to repay $25.00 of the bank loan. We want a good relationship with our banker. You hope you'll never be labeled a "bad debt." So, you take $25.00 out of our cigar box.

You bike to the bank and find the loan officer you dealt with before. "Here's $25.00 on the loan," you say. "I did really good selling lemonade and I want to pay you back. Thanks a lot!"

The bank seems pleased as you hand over the money. But something tells you that the banker isn't done yet.

"Is there something else?" you ask.

"How about the interest?" replies the banker.

"Oh, yeah," you say. "Mom and Dad said something about that. I remember when I repaid the money I borrowed from my Mom and Dad they wanted a hug," you add. "Do you want a hug, too? Is that interest?"

The banker doesn't want a hug. What the banker wants is real interest.

"Interest?" you say. "Boy, how much interest?"

"Two dollars," the banker says.

"Two dollars?! My parents just wanted a hug, they didn't charge any interest. But you want interest instead?"

The banker nods very slowly.

"Okay," you sigh, reaching into your pocket for the two dollars. "I'll pay the interest. This must be the real world. Well, thanks for taking an interest in my business."

So, what goes out in cash? *$27.00*

On the right side, let's take $27.00 out of the Notes Payable! *No!*

Why not?

Because $25 is for the principal on the Note and $2 is for what? *Interest expense.*

What do you have to reduce by $2 on the right side, to account for the interest expense. *$2 off Earnings Week to Date.*

So, the interest is a cost of doing business with whom? *The bank.*

And a cost of doing business is an expense which reduces what? *Earnings.*

Show these transactions on the next scorecard.

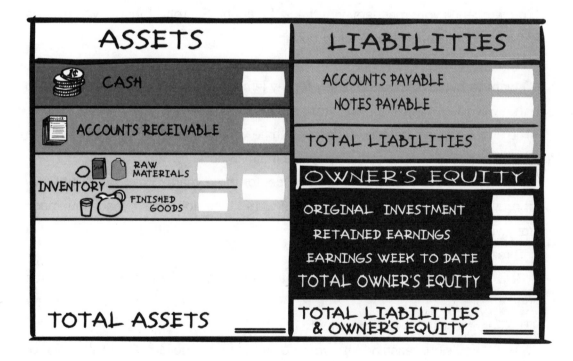

So, hey! We had to pay out some extra money to do business with the bank.

What part of this transaction shows up on our Income Statement? The Interest Expense for $2.

The interest expense shows up on the Income Statement. But not borrowing the cash or paying back the principal of the loan. It's the extra money or the cost of doing business with the bank—that expense shows up on our Income Statement.

This is important, and worth repeating. Interest expense shows up on the Income Statement as an expense.

You get another lesson about the real world when your neighbors, the ones renting you space on their lawn, become concerned with all the kids and their bikes and skateboards and roller blades around on their sidewalk and front lawn. They asked you to talk with your parents about buying an insurance policy.

Your parents agree that an insurance policy is a good idea. They agree to drive you to their insurance agent's office.

You enter the All-Safe Farm Insurance office. The agent greets you and gives you a desk calendar before you even sit down. It has large color pictures of things like red barns, mountains, forests in autumn, and kittens. It's not exactly to your taste, but, remembering your manners, you thank the agent. Secretly, though, you plan on giving it to your friend's little sister to cut up.

"Now, what can I do for you?" the agent asks.

"I want to buy an insurance policy for my lemonade business," you say. "I need one that will cover me just for the summer. Can I buy one just for this year?"

The agent says it's best to buy one for three years. In fact, he adds, he only has a three-year policy which costs $3 payable in advance.

"You mean I have to pay now, in advance, for three years?" you say. "But I only want one for this year because who knows what I'll be doing next year. How much is it anyway?"

"Three dollars," the agent tells you.

"Boy," you say, "that seems like a lot to have to buy one in advance for three years…"

The agent insists it's the only way to go.

"Okay," you sigh, reaching into your pocket for three dollars. "Here's the $3 for the policy and be sure to come by the lemonade stand. After all, I gave you some business. It's only fair that you give me some, too!"

So you give the agent how much? $3.00.

And you get what? An insurance policy.

An insurance policy especially designed just for lemonade stands. And don't forget that free, attractive desk calendar!

And this policy is going to cover you for how many years? Three years.

So now you have got this policy? Does it have value? Yes.

You have it now, right? It's something you now have for your business. So, where does it show up? On the Balance Sheet.

Where? On the Asset side.

What goes out? Cash.

How much? $3.00.

And what comes in? An insurance policy.

Did we pay for it in advance? Yes.

For how many years? Three.

How much per year? One dollar.

It's an expense then, that you paid in advance. So, what should we call this item? How about PREPAID EXPENSE.

For how much? $3.00.

Now we have a Prepaid Expense, the insurance, for $3.00.

Please record these transactions.

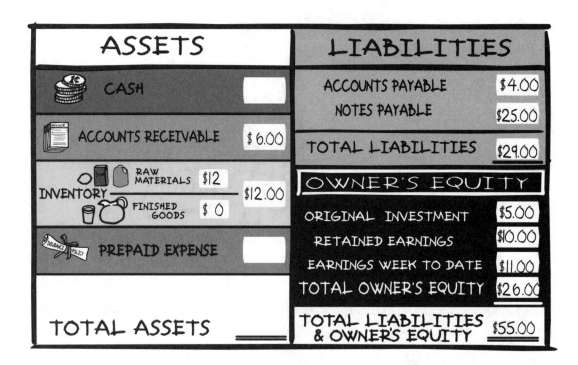

Each time we've talked about expenses, we've said they reduce earnings. What makes an expense an Asset? When we pay in advance and it has value INTO future accounting periods.

This is a special policy designed just for lemonade stands. What's going to happen to the first year when we buy this policy? Right, it's going to get used up!

So how do we reflect that on our scorecards?

The first year is a Current Expense.

So what do we do? Take one dollar off the Prepaid Expense.

Subtract ONE dollar from the prepaid expense. This year's insurance gets used up. So a dollar goes out.

Are we in balance now? No!

So, what needs to happen on the right side of the board? We take a dollar out of Earnings Week to Date.

Enter these transactions below.

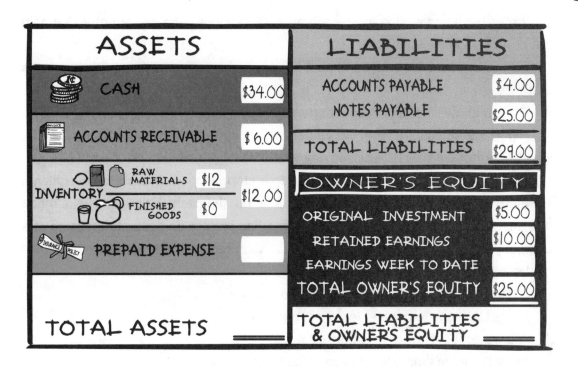

Why do we take $1.00 out of earnings? Because it's a current expense.

We paid three dollars for how many years? Three years.

For how much per year? One dollar per year.

If we go back to the agency and say we've decided to get out of the lemonade business, our insurance agent's going to give us back how much? $2.00. So a Prepaid Expense has value and is an Asset.

The policy right now is worth how much? $2.00. Right!

For which years? Year 2 + year 3.

Have we used those years yet? No.

And the ONE dollar we're taking when? Now. As a current expense.

What happens next year? Another dollar goes out.

And the next year? Still another dollar goes out.

In truth, we've taken some liberties in how we did this. Would we expense the whole first year's expense of $1 all at once? No. Since we're operating on a weekly basis, we'd take how much each week? 1/52. Right! But we're not going to mess with change at the moment, so we're going to take the whole first year's expense all at once, even though you'd expense in reality a little bit each month, or each week.

Okay. Now, for the last few pages, we've been using a very, very, very specific method of accounting.

We've been accounting for everything as it happens, whether or not we've paid out or received any what? Cash.

So, we account for everything as it happens—or, as accountants would say, as it accrues.

Do you know what this accounting method is called? The ACCRUAL METHOD.

Right, the Accrual Method. We've been accounting for everything as it happens, whether or not we paid or received any what? Cash.

The Accrual Method started when people stopped paying cash for everything. Business promises and agreements took place, but the cash settlements were made at a later date. The Accrual Method of accounting creates an accurate measure of a company's financial position even though the cash has not been settled.

Let's look at this a little closer.

Did you receive any cash for our accounts receivable? No.

Did you sell the lemonade to your friends? Yes.

Are we accounting for it as a sale? Yes.

At this point in time does it have value? Yes.

Did you earn this money? Yes.

You just didn't receive any...what? Cash.

So, on the Accrual Method, sales are recognized not as the money is received but when it is what? Earned.

How about the inventory?

Did we get the sugar? Yes.

Did we pay cash for it? No.

But we did what? Charged it—put it on account.

Did this purchase happen? Yes.

Do you owe Pappy Parker, the grocer? Yes.

Did we record that you owe it? Yes.

So, on the Accrual Method, we account for purchases when they happen or when we owe them, not when we pay for them.

Let's look at the Prepaid Expense.

How much did the insurance policy cost? $3.00 in cash.

Did we use up all $3.00 worth of insurance this year? No.

How much of the insurance happens this year or how much did we actually use this year? $1.00.

Right, we only used $1.00 of the insurance. So we account for the insurance as it happens or as we use it.

So, in the Accrual Method of accounting, we account for everything when we... Earn it.

Or when we...Owe it.

Or when we...Use it.

So, you're accounting for everything as it accrues or as it happens.

This accounting method is called what? The Accrual Method.

And on the accrual method you account for everything when? When it happens. Whether or not you've paid or received any...Cash.

One more time, on the Accrual Method you account on transaction when...? You earn it, owe it, or use it.

Great! Let's take a snapshot of our scorecard—and, while we're at it, a motion picture clip, too. It's the end of your second week in the lemonade business.

Here is a reprint of your final Balance Sheet.

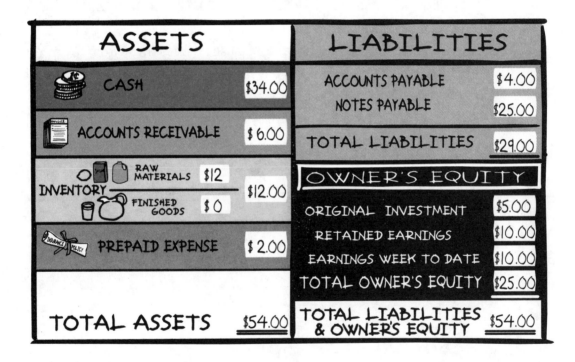

Now, using the Accrual Method of accounting, you're going to fill out your own Income Statement on page 63. But first you need more information.

And, to put it all in one place, here's information about this week's purchases, sales and expenses that you'll need to complete the income statement.

1. After a successful first week in the lemonade biz you decide to go to the bank. You show the banker your financial statements and the bank loans you $50.00 Cash.

2. You decide to give yourself an afternoon off, and sell your remaining inventory to your best friend $2.00 at cost, for Cash. Your sale, at cost = $2.00.

3. With your Inventory reduced to zero, you purchase 10 lbs. of sugar @ 40¢/lb., and charge it to the grocer on account for $4.00.

4. You purchase 100 lemons @ 20¢/lemon, paying cash $20.00.

5. You make up one batch of lemonade (50 lemons + 5 lbs. of sugar = 60 glasses). You also pay $1.00 labor to make the lemonade. Cost of Production = $13.00.

6. Sales are good. You sell all 60 glasses for 50¢ each, 40 glasses Cash and 20 glasses on account. Your Sales = $30.00, $20.00 Cash, and $10.00 in Accounts Receivable.

7. One customer who had bought 8 glasses moves away from town. You conclude that he's unlikely to pay his debt. Bad Debt Expense = $4.00.

8. You repay $25.00 of the bank loan, plus $2.00 for interest expense.

9. You pay $3.00 for a 3-year liability insurance policy. Reflect this year's insurance expense for $1.00.

Go line by line from 1 to 9, looking for these three things:

Is it a Sale?

Is it a Purchase? OR

Is it an Expense?

Your decision should help you complete the Income Statement.

There is one item that you need to fill out on your Income Statement that you won't find on the balance sheet and you won't find it in the list of transactions we just went through. Do you know what it is?...Beginning Inventory.

Now, this latest Balance Sheet is for which week? Right, week number 2.

It's not a Beginning Balance Sheet, it's a what? Ending Balance Sheet! Good.

The inventory we have left at the end of this second week is...? Ending Inventory.

Let's look at this for a moment because it's important.

We finished week two with how much ending inventory? Twelve dollars.

So we know that the Beginning Inventory for week three will be how much? Right, $12. Because the Ending Inventory always becomes the Beginning Inventory next week.

Is the Beginning Inventory for week two handy? Where could you find it? The Ending Balance Sheet from week one.

Here is week one's Ending Balance sheet for easy reference:

WEEK ONE-ENDING BALANCE SHEET

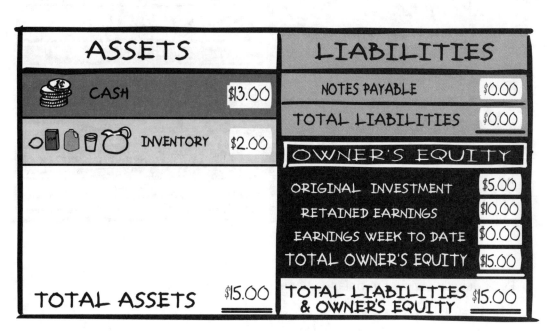

ASSETS		LIABILITIES	
CASH	$13.00	NOTES PAYABLE	$0.00
		TOTAL LIABILITIES	$0.00
INVENTORY	$2.00	OWNER'S EQUITY	
		ORIGINAL INVESTMENT	$5.00
		RETAINED EARNINGS	$10.00
		EARNINGS WEEK TO DATE	$0.00
		TOTAL OWNER'S EQUITY	$15.00
TOTAL ASSETS	$15.00	TOTAL LIABILITIES & OWNER'S EQUITY	$15.00

What was the Beginning Inventory for week number two? Two dollars.

And where did you go to find the $2? On last week's Ending Balance Sheet, The Ending Inventory.

So, you always go to the Ending Balance Sheet from the last week to find your Beginning Inventory for this week.

One more time. The ending inventory automatically becomes what? The Beginning Inventory for the Next Week.

Good. Now we're wrapping up our second week. Where do you find your Ending Inventory for week two? On week two's Ending Balance Sheet.

Okay. Good. Here's that ending balance sheet.

WEEK TWO-ENDING BALANCE SHEET

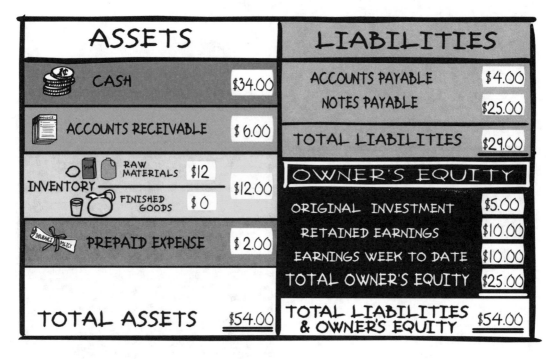

ASSETS		LIABILITIES	
CASH	$34.00	ACCOUNTS PAYABLE	$4.00
		NOTES PAYABLE	$25.00
ACCOUNTS RECEIVABLE	$6.00	TOTAL LIABILITIES	$29.00
INVENTORY — RAW MATERIALS $12 / FINISHED GOODS $0	$12.00	OWNER'S EQUITY	
		ORIGINAL INVESTMENT	$5.00
		RETAINED EARNINGS	$10.00
PREPAID EXPENSE	$2.00	EARNINGS WEEK TO DATE	$10.00
		TOTAL OWNER'S EQUITY	$25.00
TOTAL ASSETS	$54.00	TOTAL LIABILITIES & OWNER'S EQUITY	$54.00

Let's quickly review the balance sheet

Assets equal? Assets = $54.00.

Liabilities + Owner's Equity equal? Liabilities + Owner's Equity = $54.00.

Does the left side equal the right side? Yes.

The left side always, always equals what? The right side.

Good job!

Now, please complete the Income Statement. And do you remember what numbers should match on the Balance Sheet and Income Statement? Net Profit should equal Earnings Week to Date. So, we know that Net Profit should end up at $10—or you've made a mistake.

ACCRUAL INCOME STATEMENT

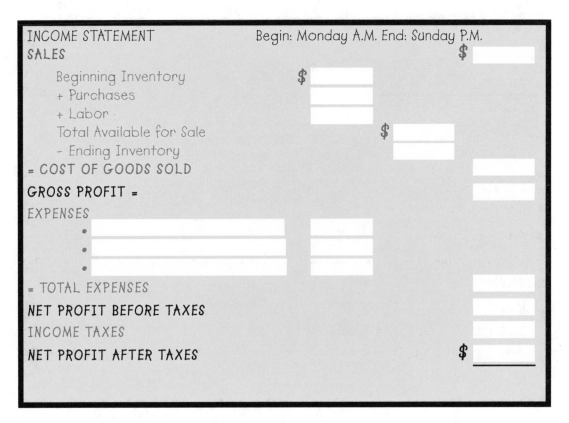

INCOME STATEMENT   Begin: Monday A.M. End: Sunday P.M.

SALES $ ____

    Beginning Inventory $ ____

    + Purchases ____

    + Labor ____

    Total Available for Sale $ ____

    - Ending Inventory ____

= COST OF GOODS SOLD ____

GROSS PROFIT = ____

EXPENSES

    • ____

    • ____

    • ____

= TOTAL EXPENSES ____

NET PROFIT BEFORE TAXES ____

INCOME TAXES ____

NET PROFIT AFTER TAXES $ ____

What were your total sales? Total Sales = $32.00

By chance, did you first have $30.00 for total sales. If so, where did the other two dollars come from? Yes, the sale to your friend at cost.

We're going to point out all the cash and non-cash items to help you better understand the Accrual Method.

To review, then:

First, we had the $2 sale. Was it Cash? Yes.

Then we had the $30 sale. How much was Cash? Twenty dollars.

And the ten dollars was what? On Account.

The Beginning Inventory was what? $2.00.

Was that Cash? No. It was lemonade.

How about purchases? $24.00

How much was cash? $20.00

And the $4 was what? Accounts Payable.

And the labor was how much? $1.00

Was it paid for with cash? Yes.

So the total available Beginning Inventory + Purchases + Labor is what? $27.00

And did we use all the Inventory? No.

What was our ending Inventory? $12.00

If we subtract that from the total available, what are the Costs of Goods Sold? $15.00

We sold the $15 worth of goods for $32 which left us how much in Gross Profit? $17.00

What were the expenses this week? Bad debt, Interest, Insurance.

The Bad Debt was what? $4.00

Did you pay Cash for that? No.

Interest was how much? $2.00.

And did we pay Cash for that? Yes.

Finally, the insurance was what? Only $1 because we are using which method of accounting? The Accrual Method.

But, did we pay Cash? Yes.

So the total expenses are? $7.00.

With a Gross Profit of $17 and $7 in expenses, what is the bottom line? $10.00.

And does this match our earnings on the Balance Sheet? Yes.

If you got $10 on the Income Statement (Net Profit) and $10 on the balance sheet (Earnings Week to Date), please give yourself a gold star!

Now, say you were just handed an Income Statement on a computer printout and you saw this 32.00 in Sales with a dollar sign next to it, your linear left brain would probably think that these total sales of $32 were all what? Cash!

But is this $32.00 all cash? No.

Some of it's what? Receivables.

But we're accounting for it as $32.00 worth of what? Sales.

But is it all cash? No.

It's cash and other things. So, it's cash and non-cash values.

And unless you went back to your sales journal and figured out what your receivables and cash sales were, you'd have no way of knowing what part of the total sales of $32.00 was Cash and what part was the Accounts Receivable.

If you just look at the $32.00, you wouldn't know what part was Cash and what part was non-cash sales.

Now, let's look at Beginning Inventory. Is inventory Cash? No.

So we had $2 worth of lemonade here.

We know we paid cash for some of our purchases and we know we charged some of our purchases. How much did we pay cash for? $20.00 And we charged...? $4.00. But when you look at this $24.00 in purchases your left brain might think again, that you paid for everything with all what? Cash.

But did you? No.

Next, you paid $1.00 cash for labor. If you look at the $15 Cost of Goods Sold, would you even know what part of that you paid cash for? And what you charged? Forget it! I can barely remember what I ate for dinner last night!

Besides, this Cost of Goods Sold...that relates only to what? Lemonade.

So, $15 in COGS is the cost of the lemons, sugar and labor that went into making up the lemonade that you sold.

And $15 from $32 gives us a Gross Profit of $17.

Now, let's look at these expenses.

Which one did we not pay cash for? Bad Debt.

So, that's not cash. We did pay cash for what? Interest and Insurance.

(By the way, you don't expense glass rental, rent, and advertising for week two because they happened last week.)

So, when we look at the $7 in total expenses; if you were looking at a financial statement and you saw $7.00 in total expenses your linear left brain again wouldn't know any better and would think you'd paid for all of these expenses with what? Cash.

But did you? No way. So, this $7 is again a mixture of Cash and non-cash expenses.

The point is, on the Accrual Method, in order to understand this method this financial statement here is treated as a "Not-Only-Cash" Income Statement. Because it has Cash and non-cash things all mixed in together. Do you know what happened in Cash here and what didn't? Not unless we have an extraordinary memory and write everything down.

You have to treat this as a "non-cash-statement" or a not-only-cash statement. By the way, this is not accounting jargon, but it's a lay person's way of remembering the Accrual Method.

Now let's look back at our Balance Sheet. Are all our Assets Cash? No. Most of the Assets are what? Non-cash things like our Accounts Receivable, Inventory, and prepaid expense.

Our total Assets are what? $54.00, and a mixture of Cash + non-cash values.

But our linear left brain might look at this $54 in total Assets and again think it was all what? Cash.

But is it? It's Cash and everything else.

So, on the Accrual Method we account for everything when it happens, whether or not we've paid or received any cash. Since it's a mixture of cash and non-cash, we call it a what?

A Not-Only-Cash method. So, there's cash and non-cash values mixed in on the accrual method.

You've probably heard the statement, "They are using creative accounting." You may think this means someone is doing something shady or illegal—but there are legitimate and legal forms of "creative accounting," and we're going to look at one now.

The Accrual Method is not the only method of keeping track of earnings. Can you guess what the other method is called? The Cash Method.

Now, let's go back and look at week number 2 using the Cash Method and we're going to need to see things very differently. We can then compare the Cash and Accrual Methods.

Some of you may want a physical way of remembering things. If so, get your finger and tie a green string (green for Cash) around it to guarantee that you will remember this forever. Repeat the following.

Cash is Cash is Cash!

Now, switch to your other hand and tie a green string around your finger and repeat again:

Cash is Cash is Cash!

So on the Cash Method you would account for things ONLY when they happen in what? Cash.

So, only events happening in cash are accounted for on the Cash Method. Remember that in the accrual method, everything is accounted for as it is earned, owed, and used.

On the Cash Method, you account for things when you receive what? Cash. And when you pay what? Cash.

The Cash Method, obviously, is very different from the Accrual Method where you Account for a transaction regardless of whether you paid or received cash. You can expect that the results will be different.

Okay. We've been on what kind of method the whole day? Accrual.

But now, we are only going to do a Cash Income Statement to show the contrast of the Cash and Accrual Methods. You will need to look back at the Accrual Method Income Statement on page 65 as you complete the Cash Method Income Statement below.

```
CASH INCOME STATEMENT          Begin: Monday A.M. End: Sunday P.M.
SALES                                                    $ [        ]

     Beginning Inventory               $ [        ]
   + Purchases                           [        ]
   + Labor                               [        ]
     Total available for sale         $ [        ]
   - Ending Inventory                    [        ]
 = COST OF GOODS SOLD                                      [        ]

GROSS PROFIT =                                            [        ]

EXPENSES
     • [                    ]           [        ]
     • [                    ]           [        ]
 = TOTAL EXPENSES                                         [        ]

NET PROFIT (Gross Profit - Expenses)                    $ [        ]
```

Let's begin with sales. What would be the total sales on the cash method? $22.00 Total Sales.

Why is it only $22, instead of the $32 on the Accrual Method? The Accounts Receivable doesn't show up.

Moving down, is Beginning Inventory cash? No. So nothing will show up there.

How much did we have in cash purchases? $20.00.

And how much in cash for labor? $1.00.

What would our Cost of Goods sold be on the Cash Method? $21.00. Right!

So, whatever, we paid Cash for is our Cost of Goods Sold!

Which means, we don't even account for what? The sugar. Why? Because we charged it.

It's not accounted for because we charged it; we didn't pay what? Cash.

So if sales are $22 and COGS is $21, what is the Gross Profit?

$1.00. WOW! All that hard work for one measly buck! No wonder some really lucky kids get their parents to send them to camp!

Let's look at Expenses:

Does the Bad Debt show up? No.

Because it's not what? Cash.

How about interest? Yes, $2.00, because you paid out cash for that.

How about the insurance? Yes. Okay, but $1.00 or $3.00?

How much did you pay out in Cash? $3.00.

So, yes, you can expense all $3 this year? Wow! Because you paid for it, with what? Cash.

So, we're going to take the whole $3 for all three years this year. We paid for it with cash in advance, so we're going to take all three years worth of expense now.

Total Expenses are $5. If Gross Profit is one dollar and Expenses are $5, what's the Net Profit. $-4.00. Yikes! This is going from bad to worse!

Let's look at these two Income Statements.

We used two methods. Did we get different results? Yes! The Accrual Method +$10 in Earnings and the cash Method was -$4.

So, you can see that businesses have an opportunity here to be creative in how they account for things. Which method would you want to use? Accrual.

Accrual, why? It looks better—to take to the bank or investors—because it has more profit.

For what other reason would you use the Accrual Method? It's more accurate—everything that happened is accounted for.

Why use the Cash Method? For tax purposes.

Oh, with minus $4 in earnings, will you owe any taxes? No. In fact, you might get some refund.

Can you use the Cash Method in our lemonade business? Good question!

Well, some businesses can use the Cash Method and some cannot. There is one item on the Balance Sheet that determines whether or not you can use the Cash Method.

What is it? Inventory.

Yes, any business with inventory must use only which method? Accrual.

Does the lemonade stand have inventory? Yes. So which method do we have to use? Accrual.

Let's look at why a company with inventory can't use the Cash Method.

At the end of every year, if we saw that we were going to make a profit and have to pay taxes, we could just run out and buy a lot of inventory and pay cash for it, and then take it all as COGS and reduce our profit so we wouldn't have to pay any taxes.

Do you think the government would like that? Since we have a business that sells inventory, do you think the government will allow us to report on the cash method? No way!

What kind of businesses can be on the Cash Method? Service business, like doctors, lawyers, accountants, seminar companies, consultants, real estate companies, cleaning services. etc.

What's the deciding factor? Inventory.

So, you mean to tell me that our lemonade stand can't report to the IRS using the Cash Method? Sorry it's the law.

What accounting method do we have to report on? Accrual.

Because we have what? Inventory.

So if you're delivering a service, the IRS says it's okay for you to be on which method? Cash.

And for those of us in manufacturing, retail, or wholesale with inventory for sale we must be on which method? Accrual.

For the sake of argument, what would happen next year if we could be on the Cash Method? On the Cash Method, we'll take $3 this year for our insurance expense.

Can we take any of the insurance next year as an expense? No. So what's going to happen? Our profit's going to go up.

So, for those service businesses that can be on the Cash Method, they take as many expenses now so they can pay less what? Taxes, right!

When will it catch up with them? Next year.

They weren't getting out of paying taxes, just what? Delaying.

Have you ever heard the saying "a tax deferred is a tax reduced"? The theory is you're going to defer taxes this year and when you do have to pay them, you'll pay for them with what kind of dollars? Cheaper or inflated. And who gets to use the money you saved by deferring taxes? You do!

So that's the game. If you're a manufacturer, can you do this? No.

What method is the most accurate reflection of reality and profitability? Accrual.

What method are we running your lemonade business on? Accrual.

Can a service company keep both sets of books?

Guess what? In the service business, we can report to the government on the Cash Method, and keep our books on the Accrual Method to show the banks or investors. Sounds like two sets of books...pretty shady! Can we have two sets of books? Yes. It's called "Creative Accounting."

Guess what happens at the end of the year? We give our books to our accountant and what does our accountant do? Turns it into the Cash Method for whom? For the IRS.

A lot of businesses run the business on the Accrual basis and submit to the government on the Cash basis for tax purposes.

Can you switch methods? Be very creative? The government will always allow a business to switch from the Cash to the Accrual Method (they will most likely collect more taxes), but you cannot switch the other way. So if you start a service company and want to use the Cash Method, you need to elect that method the first year.

What about service companies that have some inventory they sell? Like a seminar company that sells books?

This can get into a gray area where there is disagreement between the business owner and the IRS. The IRS will ask, "Is the inventory material to the generation of profit to the business?" If the answer is "yes," then you have to use the Accrual Method. If "no," you can use the Cash Method. The gray area is how much is "material to generating profit" and most businesses would consult its Certified Public Accountant (CPA) on this issue, but it doesn't take much.

Before closing this chapter, let's review it.

On the Accrual Method you account for things when? When they happen.

When you earn it and when you...what? Owe it.

Or when you? Use it.

Whether or not you've paid or received any what? Cash.

And on the Cash Method, cash is cash is cash.

And you only account for things when they happen in cash or when you what? Pay it or receive it.

PHEW!

You're doing great! Take a break before we move on the next bit of business!

CHAPTER 5

$\mathcal{I}$t's only been two weeks that you've been in the lemonade business, and already your fame is spreading!

The local neighborhood newspaper ran an article about you on page five! There you were, photographed at the lemonade stand, proud as punch....Okay, maybe make that proud as lemonade! The article quoted your mom and dad saying how it was all your idea and how proud they are of you. It quoted Pappy Parker saying he wished there were more kids like you. It quoted a few kids who said your lemonade was the best they've ever tasted—and they weren't even your friends!

You're trying not to get a swelled head over all of this. After all, it's not like you saved the world or something really important. Still, some of the neighborhood kids start coming to you for advice about starting their own lemonade businesses. "Wow, should I do this?" you ask yourself. You have to consider your own business. These kids are asking you to help create competition for yourself. You decide you will definitely not work with anyone near enough to open a stand in your own neighborhood.

The phone keeps ringing off the hook with kids wanting your help in starting their businesses. The demand is such that—being a genius on your good days—you realize this means that to do this you have to start a second business yourself! But you're only one person. How can you run both your own lemonade stand and a consulting business? Do you really want to expand? Do you want to become a consultant?

Finally, you realize that you need some consulting yourself, so you call your favorite aunt, Jane, for some advice. Aunt Jane has run her own management consulting firm for years. How will I be able to run two businesses is your question for Jane. Your aunt says you will have to hire some friends and let them start out running the stand and you can train them to be consultants. Your next question is, "Should I combine my financial records for the consulting firm with the lemonade stand financial statements or set up a separate business?"

Jane says that you can do either, but reminds you that consulting is a different kind of business—it's a service business. You immediately remember what we all learned in the last chapter—services businesses do not have inventory and can gain a tax advantage by using the Cash Method of accounting for reporting to the IRS. You figure that's for you and decide to start a second business—the Real Good Lemonade Consulting Company.

Next you ask Aunt Jane how to charge for your consulting services. She starts talking about "billable hours" and you say, "Huh?" What she means is that service businesses are all about managing and optimizing the use of time. At the lemonade stand you have to manage your product, lemonade, and your time, but a consultant's only inventory is his or her time. Aunt Jane says that what this means is you don't make money unless you are doing something that you can bill to the customer. You need to come up with an hourly or daily billing rate.

You ask Jane if the Balance Sheet and Income Statement are different for a service business. Jane asks you to get out a Balance Sheet from your lemonade stand. She is impressed by how well organized you are and particularly by your innovation of using color to help understand the Balance Sheet items. She asks you what is the one item on your lemonade stand Balance Sheet that will not be on a service company's Balance Sheet. "Inventory," you tell her. (You love easy questions!) That's the only difference if you are using the Accrual Method of accounting.

Aunt Jane says the Income Statement is a different story. She says that since there is no Ending Inventory to subtract out of costs, services companies really only have Sales and Expenses. That makes it really easy to do your Income Statement. You start to feel agitated.

"Aunt Jane," you say, "wouldn't a service company want to separate its overhead costs to run the daily operation from its direct costs?"

She can't believe how smart you are. She promises you a future job on the spot.

Aunt Jane says that, indeed, most service companies separate costs into two categories—Cost of Services and Expenses. Cost of Services are the costs directly related to providing a service. Expenses are all the overhead costs or costs to run the business, just like in our lemonade stand.

As we noted earlier, the structure of such a service company's Income Statement would be:

Sales

- Cost of Services

= Gross Profit

- Expenses

= Net Profit

Many of you reading this book either work in service companies or for large companies with inventory that have service divisions. The purpose of this chapter is to help you better understand service company issues and accounting and give you a chance to do some practice determining which items go into Cost of Services (some people call it Cost of Sales) and which into Expense. We will get back to our lemonade stand in the next chapter. Please don't confuse what we are doing in this brief chapter on service businesses with your lemonade stand business. The numbers here will not affect what we've done earlier. It's a question of apples and oranges—or lemons!

Since the Balance Sheets for the two types of companies are the same (except for Inventory), we will not focus on the Balance Sheet at all in this chapter.

Now, let's pretend to shoot forward in time a couple of months. You did hire some friends who learned your business's core competencies rapidly helping you out at the lemonade stand.

Thanks to the article in the local newspaper and great word of mouth, your new consulting business and its two employees get busy in a hurry. Encouraged by this response, you take out a classified ad for the business. Your younger brother, Michael, wants to get involved, so you promise him a $1 sales commission on any contract he brings into the business.

Okay, let's go consult!

Hot after sales leads, Michael sends the newspaper article to your dad's half sister, Sue (I know—complex family structures—it's the modern world), and her husband, Eric. They have two kids, your cousins, Amanda and Laura, who want to start a lemonade stand and be just like you. Aunt Sue thinks this is hilarious, since Amanda is always complaining when her younger sister Laura tries to copy her. Still, she wants to help them—and you. Who knows? Maybe in the process all of you will learn important lessons.

You sell Aunt Sue three days of consulting for two consultants at $8 per day for each consultant and include all travel costs in the daily rate. They live in the next town which is 30 miles away, requiring two overnights in a local hotel for your two consultants. Luckily, your employees' parents volunteer to go along and pay for the hotel. The cost for travel (gas for cars) comes to $6. Plus, you pay the consultants $2.00 per day for every day they work with clients.

Your younger brother, Michael, agrees to do the administrative work for the contract and other office tasks. You pay him $2 for the week. You also give him the $1 sales commission he earned by selling this job to Aunt Sue.

Since the newspaper article brought you such a good response, you decide to continue the ad in the next issue. Advertising the new business costs $4.

Your two consultants work Monday, Tuesday, and Wednesday with the clients (your cousins). They take along $2 worth of lemons and $1 worth of sugar to demonstrate how to make lemonade, in case your cousins decide to go with your amazing, awesome, totally appetizing secret recipe. (Hey, if McDonald's can franchise, why can't you?!)

On Thursday, back home, they work all day developing a new consulting product for your Real Good Lemonade Consulting Company to sell. (It's a leadership course for shy kids called, "DON'T BE SHY—GET THEM TO BUY!"). You only pay the consultants $1.50 per day when they are working at the office.

On Friday, they performed general and administrative tasks at the office (your basement playroom).

Now, it's time to practice. Using the above transactions, complete the following Income Statement for the Real Good Lemonade Consulting Company. Your main task is to determine which items go into Cost of Services and which go into Expenses.

Remember, Cost of Services is any cost directly related to providing the service and Expenses are all the cost of doing business not directly related to providing the service.

SERVICE BUSINESS INCOME STATEMENT

SALES

Cost of Services (Cost of Sales)

TOTAL COST OF SERVICES

GROSS PROFIT

Expenses

TOTAL EXPENSE

NET PROFIT

Okay, let's see how you did.

The client (Aunt Sue and Uncle Eric) bought three days at $8/day per consultant. You sent two consultants. So, what was the total revenue? $48.00

What did you put into Cost of Services? Well, you had to pay your consultants $2.00/day times 2 consultants times 3 days = $12.00 You had to pay for their travel costs ($6.00). They took along $3.00 worth of product which was used for demonstration purposes and left with the client.

So, your Cost of Services are? $21.00.

Following our formula, subtracting Cost of Services from Sales leaves you with a Gross Profit (Income) of...? $27.00.

Now, what items were in Expenses? Remember, Expenses are costs not directly related to the delivery of services.

You paid Michael a sales commission ($1.00) and paid for some advertising in the newspaper ($4.00).

Michael also did the administrative work for the contract and other office tasks ($2.00). Then, on Friday, your consultants, each earning $1.50, spent the day performing administrative tasks at your office. (They claim they were busy with paperwork, though you suspect mostly they played Solitaire on your family's computer.)

There's one more expense. How much did DON'T BE SHY—GET THEM TO BUY! cost you to develop? $3.00 for Research and Development.

So, what are the total expenses? $13.00.

We're almost done. Last thing, subtracting Expenses from Gross Income leaves us with a Net Income of...? $14.00.

Now, you may be wondering about a few things. One may be how we handled the sales commission. Some of you may want sales commission to go in Cost of Services, since you can argue that it is a direct cost of the sale. But is it truly a part of the cost of delivering the service? Not really. Because of this, many businesses put sales commission in Expenses. Either way you did it is okay by accounting standards and by the IRS. What is required is that you be consistent in how it's reported.

Travel costs may be another area you're wondering about. Travel costs are in Cost of Services because they are part of delivering the services by contract. Most real-life consulting companies make the client reimburse any and all travel costs. If travel is reimbursed dollar for dollar, it is handled as a non-revenue item in a separate account.

How come your employees' wages show up in different categories? Because consultants' wages are in Cost of Services only when they are working on a project. Their relative time as consultants, doing administrative tasks, and R&D lets us know how efficiently we are using their time (which is the only source of the consulting company's revenue). Not all service companies have R&D, but for those that do, separating it allows you to keep track of how much capital investment goes into new products. This is helpful in determining how to price them.

Review your Income Statement again. Does anything concern you? What are potential problem areas? How would you improve this company's profitability?

Remember we said earlier that time is the critical issue in a service company. You might question the wisdom of using the consultants for administrative tasks. Their salaries are much higher than Michael's for performing these tasks. Lots of service companies get into financial difficulties when they end up having too much time when their services providers are not working directly for clients on "billable hours."

What else haven't we covered in this brief side trip? Certain types of expenses, for one. Interest expense, other expenses, and taxes would have to be subtracted to arrive at the true bottom line after taxes. You may wonder what "other expenses" mean. These are things like a loss or gain from selling a fixed asset (which we haven't done).

Well, we certainly haven't exhausted a discussion about service businesses and how to treat them accounting-wise. But, hopefully, you know some of the things to keep in mind if you're in a service business. Below is our Income Statement with the major categories used by typical service companies.

REAL GOOD LEMONADE COMPANY INCOME STATEMENT		
SALES		$48.00
COST OF SERVICES		$21.00
GROSS PROFIT		$27.00
Expenses		
Sales and Marketing	$5.00	
General and Administrative	$5.00	
Research and Development	$3.00	
TOTAL EXPENSE		$13.00
NET PROFIT		$14.00

You like having a second business. Maybe one day you'll sell your lemonade stand and concentrate on being a consultant full-time. For now, though, you enjoy making a product and selling it. So, let's leave the consulting world for a while and return to the best-tasting lemonade in the whole wide world!

After all, week three is about to begin!

CHAPTER 6

$O O O$

Okay, we're ready to start week number three. Stop and consider how much we've already learned about accounting! With all the knowledge we've gained so far, the coming week promises to be our best ever. Hmmm…maybe next summer, we'll let someone else run the lemonade stand and we'll promote ourselves to financial geniuses and become one of those big bucks consultants.

Certainly, dreaming of a glorious future is part of being in business. But, it's Monday morning, and it's time to return to reality. This summer we're running a lemonade stand.

At breakfast, you glance at the newspaper. The weather forecast promises a hot and sunny week. Great! But you don't need the newspaper to tell you that there's a clear, beautiful blue sky outside. Or that, thanks to the warm air, birds are chirping and singly loudly. Finishing your breakfast, you can practically feel the grass, flowers, and leaves growing outside! Boy, it's great being alive!

Yes, you're definitely hot for another successful week in business! But, before we start, what do we need to do?

Roll up the earnings! (Move last week's earnings into Retained Earnings.)

Please do so now.

BEGINNING BALANCE SHEET—WEEK THREE

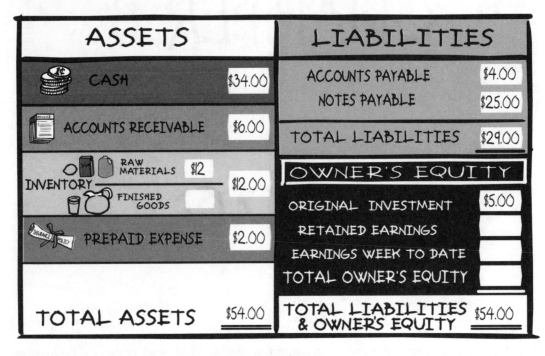

ASSETS		LIABILITIES	
CASH	$34.00	ACCOUNTS PAYABLE	$4.00
		NOTES PAYABLE	$25.00
ACCOUNTS RECEIVABLE	$6.00	TOTAL LIABILITIES	$29.00
INVENTORY RAW MATERIALS $12 FINISHED GOODS	$12.00	OWNER'S EQUITY	
		ORIGINAL INVESTMENT	$5.00
PREPAID EXPENSE	$2.00	RETAINED EARNINGS	
		EARNINGS WEEK TO DATE	
		TOTAL OWNER'S EQUITY	
TOTAL ASSETS	$54.00	TOTAL LIABILITIES & OWNER'S EQUITY	$54.00

So, it's a new Monday, and time to replenish your inventory of raw materials. Even though you still have 50 lemons and 5 pounds of sugar left over from last week, you think that more will be needed for this week's sales. You get your bike out of the garage, jump on, and (checking for cars, of course) cruise down the street. You're heading toward Pappy Parker's neighborhood grocery store. You're feeling like a seasoned and savvy entrepreneur. After all, you've worked really hard the past few weeks. As a reward, you promise yourself a bottle of juice, some doughnuts, and a candy bar for later.

But, when you reach the store, you're in a shock. There would be no extra money for treats because the price of lemons has doubled to 40 cents a piece!

This is an outrage! Someone should call the President! Or, at least, the governors of Florida and California, where the lemons come from. What's going on here? Is someone trying to run you out of business?

You can't make lemonade without lemons, though. You want 50 lemons, but you didn't bring enough money to pay cash. You complain about the price to Pappy. He isn't happy about the price increase, either. "I'm paying more, too. Apparently, a freak storm destroyed a lot of the lemon crop," Pappy explains. "No one's getting rich from the disaster."

The explanation calms you some. "We lemon people must stick together—or, maybe, squeeze together in tough times," you tell good ol' Pappy.

He nods. "Listen, I'll be happy to sell you these lemons on account. Should I add $20.00 to what you have on credit?"

"Please," you say with a nod. "Mr. Parker, you're the nicest man in the whole world—except for my dad, of course—and my uncles and grandpas."

Riding home, you feel happy that Pappy is such a nice person. You feel sorry for those lemon farmers who lost their crop. But, mostly, you feel sorry for yourself that the cost of lemons just doubled.

When you get home, you do a new Balance Sheet.

You ask yourself, what comes in? Inventory.

Inventory for how much? $20.00.

Did you pay cash for it? No. We charged it.

Demonstrate the transaction on the next Balance Sheet.

Are we in balance? No.

What do we have to do? Increase Accounts Payable.

Increase Accounts Payable by how much? $20.00

Now, are we in balance? Yes.

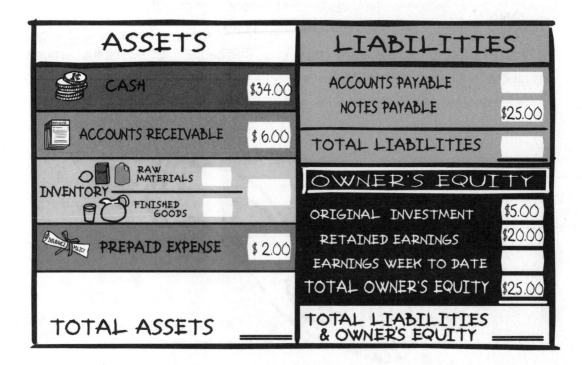

But, there's something else. Look at Inventory. We now need a way to separate the 50 lemons @ 20 cents each from the 50 lemons @ 40 cents each.

Okay, so let's take a look at our Inventory. Do we have lemons in Inventory at two different costs? Yes.

Right now, we have 100 lemons, and 50 of them cost 20 cents each and the other 50 cost 40 cents each. Can that happen in any business with inventory—you buy the same raw material but at different costs? Yes. The price of raw materials can shift without any notice. Which means that you could buy the same material but at any number of different costs.

You start to think, Hmmmmm. Soon, I'm going to make another batch of lemonade using 50 lemons. What will be the cost of the lemons? Well, ah, either, you know...some at, like you said, 20 cents and others at, well, 40 cents. Just please don't ask me which price lemons are going into the next batch!

It can get confusing, can't it? Well, the decision our business makes about how to value its inventory is what we will look at now.

We live in America, and, as you might guess, some enterprising entrepreneur once saw this issue and came up with a way for all businesses with inventory to be creative.

We're going to first look at a method of valuing our inventory where the first lemons that come into the stand are the first lemons that go out.

First in, first out. FIFO. What does this stand for?

Simply stated, it means that the first lemons that came in will be the first lemons that go out, or the first lemons that we sell.

Here's another way to took at FIFO.

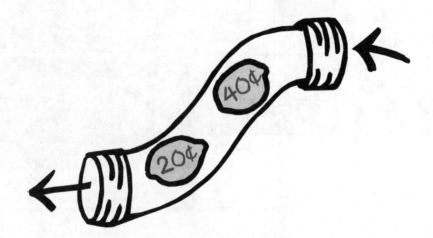

Pretend you are putting the lemons in a pipeline, in the order that you purchased them. So, which lemons are first in the pipeline? The 20 cent ones. And, which are the last in? The 40 cent ones.

Good, so make up another batch of lemonade—remember our recipe? Five pounds of sugar + 50 lemons = 60 glasses. (For your information, sugar is 40 cents a pound.) You make this batch yourself, so there's no labor charge.

What is the COST OF PRODUCTION using FIFO:

$ _____

So, using FIFO, how much do the lemons cost? Ten dollars.

You take the cost of the "first-in" lemons, which is 20¢ per lemon—for a total of $10. Then add five pounds of sugar at 40¢/lb., for a total of $2. Get these raw materials (lemons and sugar) and mix them up real good in your pitcher—because it's time to sell some lemonade!

But, first, demonstrate these transactions on a new Balance Sheet.

ASSETS		LIABILITIES	
CASH	$34.00	ACCOUNTS PAYABLE	$24.00
		NOTES PAYABLE	$25.00
ACCOUNTS RECEIVABLE	$6.00	TOTAL LIABILITIES	$49.00
INVENTORY — RAW MATERIALS		OWNER'S EQUITY	
FINISHED GOODS		ORIGINAL INVESTMENT	$5.00
		RETAINED EARNINGS	$20.00
PREPAID EXPENSE	$2.00	EARNINGS WEEK TO DATE	$0.00
		TOTAL OWNER'S EQUITY	$25.00
TOTAL ASSETS		TOTAL LIABILITIES & OWNER'S EQUITY	$74.00

Maybe you're feeling a bit challenged by all the important accounting concepts and practices you're learning. But you're doing great! Better yet, there are no challenges to selling your lemonade today!

It's hot and people are lined up at your lemonade stand. The word of mouth about your great tasting lemonade has spread—and there are lots of new customers in addition to your regular ones.

"Say, kid," a grownup wearing a suit says, "I'll give you one hundred dollars for your secret recipe."

"No chance!" you say. "Where would Coca-Cola be if it sold its recipe years ago? Sorry, a hundred dollars is not enough."

Business is great all week long! You sell all the glasses for 50 cents each. Fifty glasses are sold for cash. Ten glasses are sold on account. Total sales = $30.00, $25.00 for Cash and $5.00 in Accounts Receivable.

Demonstrate the day's transaction on the next Balance Sheet.

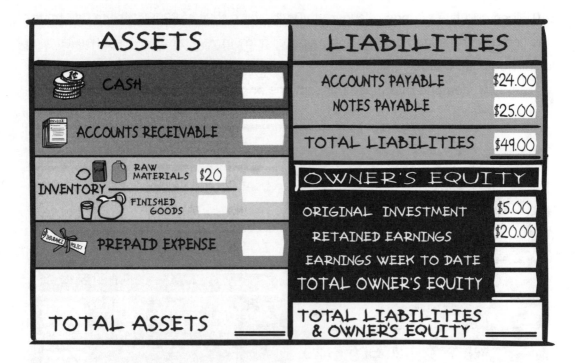

Let's review what you just did.

First, what goes out of our business? Inventory.

How much Inventory $12.00

What comes in? Cash.

Okay, so bring in the Cash. How much Cash? $25.00

And then what else comes in? Accounts Receivable for $5.00

Are we in balance yet? No. The Assets are $92 and the right side equals $74.00

We just made some more Profit, right?

What was the sale? $30.00

What did it cost us? $12.00

What are the Earnings Week to Date? $18.00 Add the earnings to the right side, to balance.

Let's go through this again.

Now, on FIFO, which cost of lemons did we use. The first ones.

What's our cost of goods? $12–$10 for lemons and $2 for sugar.

Which cost of lemons did we leave on the books? The last lemons.

Okay, we used 20¢ lemons and left the 40¢ lemons on the books in inventory.

Now, we're at the end of the week.

What we want to do is look at different ways of valuing Inventory. Since all we want to do is isolate the inventory, let's avoid bringing in any expenses this week. Normally, in a business, would we have expenses every week? Yes.

Right now, though, we just want to look at different ways of valuing our inventory. Okay?

To do this, let's examine the week-end Balance Sheet and Income Statement. Here's your latest Balance Sheet, filled out for your convenience.

ACCRUAL FIFO BALANCE SHEET

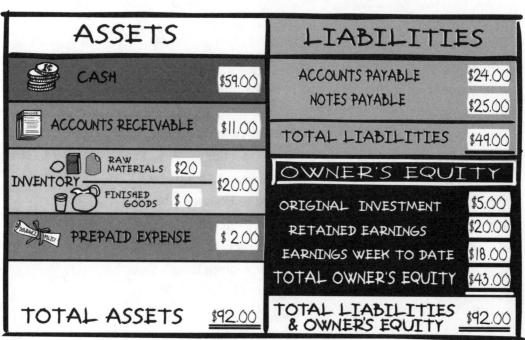

ASSETS		LIABILITIES	
CASH	$59.00	ACCOUNTS PAYABLE	$24.00
		NOTES PAYABLE	$25.00
ACCOUNTS RECEIVABLE	$11.00	TOTAL LIABILITIES	$49.00
INVENTORY — RAW MATERIALS $20 — FINISHED GOODS $0	$20.00	OWNER'S EQUITY	
		ORIGINAL INVESTMENT	$5.00
		RETAINED EARNINGS	$20.00
PREPAID EXPENSE	$2.00	EARNINGS WEEK TO DATE	$18.00
		TOTAL OWNER'S EQUITY	$43.00
TOTAL ASSETS	$92.00	TOTAL LIABILITIES & OWNER'S EQUITY	$92.00

Does the left side equal the right side? It sure does.

Since this is the end of the week, this Balance Sheet is an Ending Balance Sheet.

Now, fill out the Income Statement below.

FIFO INCOME STATEMENT

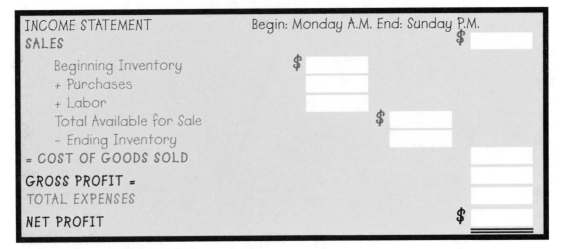

Sales were what? $30.00

Beginning Inventory? $12.00

Purchases? $20.00

Ending Inventory? $20.00

Total available for sale? $32.00

So, our Cost of Goods Sold was what? $12.00

Which makes our Gross Profit what? $18.00

And, remember, we're not going to show any Expenses—so that's zero. Which means that our Net Profit is how much? $18.00

Does your Net Profit on the Income Statement match your Earnings Week to Date on the Balance Sheet? It should. If you got $18.00 on both, give yourself a pat on the back!

So, this week on FIFO, which cost of lemons did we use? Twenty cent lemons.

Which is the cost of the lemons left on the Balance Sheet? Forty cent ones.

We said earlier that there were different systems to value our inventory. We just used FIFO to develop the week's financial records. But, now, let's go through the transactions a second time, using the other system to value our Inventory.

Let's redo the week. Instead of First In, First Out (FIFO), we will use the opposite method of valuing inventory, which is Last In, First Out (LIFO).

Remember, we purchased 50 lemons on account. The price had just increased to forty cents a lemon. Let's start from this transaction.

What comes in? Inventory.

For how much? $20.00.

Do you pay cash? No.

So, to make the balance sheet balance, you need to increase what? Accounts Payable.

By how much? $20.00.

Remember, this time we will have the same Balance Sheet as on page 83, but we're using the LIFO system of valuing our Inventory.

ASSETS		LIABILITIES	
CASH	$34.00	ACCOUNTS PAYABLE	$24.00
		NOTES PAYABLE	$25.00
ACCOUNTS RECEIVABLE	$6.00	TOTAL LIABILITIES	$49.00
INVENTORY — RAW MATERIALS $32 / FINISHED GOODS $0	$32.00	OWNER'S EQUITY	
		ORIGINAL INVESTMENT	$5.00
		RETAINED EARNINGS	$20.00
PREPAID EXPENSE	$2.00	EARNINGS WEEK TO DATE	$0.00
		TOTAL OWNER'S EQUITY	$25.00
TOTAL ASSETS	$74.00	TOTAL LIABILITIES & OWNER'S EQUITY	$74.00

We're using the system where the last-in lemons will be the first lemons that go out—that we sell. The last lemons that come in will be the first lemons out. What is this method called? LIFO. Which means what? Last in, first out.

The pipeline metaphor won't work this time. Instead, let's pretend we're putting the lemons in a barrel.

Which lemons are on the bottom? The 20 cent lemons. **And which are on the top?** The 40 cent lemons. **Yes, and the last ones in are the first ones out.**

Good. Now, make up another batch of lemonade: 5 pounds of sugar plus 50 lemons (and 2 gallons of water) make 60 glasses of lemonade.

If we make up this batch of lemonade using the LIFO system, what is the cost of the lemons? $20.00. **So, the lemons cost what?** $20.00. **Plus the sugar, which is how much?** $2.00. **So, what is the cost of production using LIFO?**

The Cost of Production using LIFO is
$_____

We'll need this in a moment, so let's repeat it. What's the cost of production using LIFO? $22.00

Demonstrate this on the next scorecard.

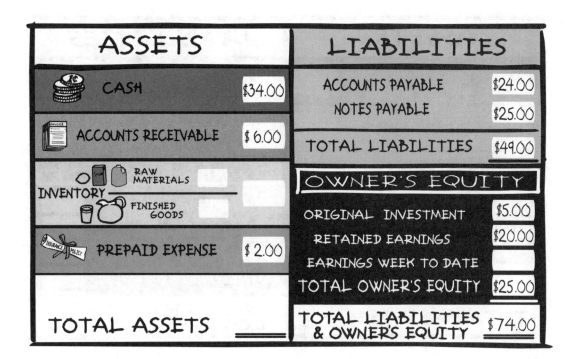

Moving on, you have a great week and sell the entire batch of 60 glasses. Again, 50 glasses for cash and 10 on account.

What goes out of the business? Inventory.

How much inventory (using LIFO)? $22.00. Remember, on LIFO, the last lemons—or the expensive, higher priced lemons—are the ones that go out. The cheaper, lower priced lemons are left where? In Ending Inventory.

How much Cash comes in? $25.00.

How much comes in as Accounts Receivable? $5.00

Let's do a new Balance Sheet.

ASSETS		LIABILITIES	
CASH		ACCOUNTS PAYABLE	
		NOTES PAYABLE	
ACCOUNTS RECEIVABLE		TOTAL LIABILITIES	
INVENTORY — RAW MATERIALS		**OWNER'S EQUITY**	
INVENTORY — FINISHED GOODS		ORIGINAL INVESTMENT	
PREPAID EXPENSE		RETAINED EARNINGS	
		EARNINGS WEEK TO DATE	
		TOTAL OWNER'S EQUITY	
TOTAL ASSETS		TOTAL LIABILITIES & OWNER'S EQUITY	

Once again, there are no Expenses for the week.

Now, show these transaction on the LIFO Income Statement.

LIFO INCOME STATEMENT

INCOME STATEMENT   Begin: Monday A.M. End: Sunday P.M.
SALES $

    Beginning Inventory $
    + Purchases
    + Labor
    Total Available for Sale $
    - Ending Inventory
= COST OF GOODS SOLD

GROSS PROFIT =
TOTAL EXPENSES

NET PROFIT $

Sales were what? $30.00.

Beginning Inventory? $12.00.

Purchases? $20.00.

Total available for sale? *$32.00.*

Ending Inventory of what? *$10.00*

Cost of Goods Sold is what? *$22.00.*

Wait a second! Twenty-two dollars in cost of goods sold? That's expensive? Why was the COGS higher? *Because the last ones in were the more expensive ones.*

Gross Profit is what? *$8.00.*

No Expenses this week, so that's zero.

Thus, our Net Profit is what? *$8.00.*

Wow! That's low, compared to FIFO.

On the LIFO method, what are the total Assets? *$82.00.*

On the LIFO method, what are the total Liabilities and Owner's Equity? *$82.00.*

Does the left side equal the right side? *Yes.*

Okay! We used two different Inventory valuation methods. Did we get different bottom lines? *Yes.*

What was our Net Profit with FIFO? *$18.00.* And what was our net profit with LIFO? *$8.00.* FIFO gives us a Net Profit that is what? *Higher.* Why was it higher with FIFO? *Because with FIFO, our Cost of Goods Sold was lower and Ending Inventory was higher.*

Fill out the following table, to make comparisons between FIFO and LIFO.

FIFO vs. LIFO—THE NUMBERS DO NOT LIE!

	FIFO	LIFO
SALES	$_____	$_____
COGS (Cost of Goods Sold)	$_____	$_____
PROFIT	$_____	$_____
ENDING INVENTORY	$_____	$_____

What conclusions can we reach?

FIFO IS LOW COG, HIGH ENDING INVENTORY HIGH NET PROFIT.

LIFO IS HIGH COG, LOW ENDING INVENTORY LOW NET PROFIT.

Remember, we said that accounting could be creative. Here is another way that businesses can be creative by how they account for what happens to their inventory.

Which method would you prefer? Well...it depends.

Yes, it depends.

What's a good reason for using FIFO? For one, it looks better on paper. FIFO gives me a better bottom line!

Good thinking! But if you make more earnings, what will the government want from you? More taxes.

So, why use LIFO? Taxes. With lower earnings, our taxes will be lower, too. Which method do you think is simpler to keep track of? FIFO. True, FIFO is easier. So, remember this, the only reason a business would choose LIFO is to SAVE TAXES!

What was that? I can't hear you!

The only reason a business would choose LIFO is to SAVE TAXES!

But, you may ask, is this always true?

That's a good question to look at.

What is happening to prices in this example that makes LIFO show lower profit and taxes? Prices are rising. True, companies and businesses with rising costs who want to pay less taxes would chose which method? LIFO.

Suppose, though, prices are falling and you still want to save taxes. Which method should you pick? FIFO.

What major industry has had falling prices over the past few years? Computers and electronics. So, companies in those industries that want to save taxes would use what inventory valuation method? FIFO.

The choice of FIFO or LIFO is an important one, which involves two criteria. What is your tax strategy? What direction are prices going in your industry? (Also, you wouldn't look at pricing in the next couple years. You'd look at the trend over a twenty-five period and try to predict the future.)

Let's look at the week's numbers, to review the two different systems.

What are total Assets on FIFO? $92.00.

And on LIFO? $82.00.

What's the difference between the two Balance Sheets? $10.00.

Where on the left side of the two Balance Sheets does the difference show up—besides the total assets? Inventory.

And where on the right side of the two balance sheets does the difference show up—besides the total Liabilities and Owner's Equity? Earnings.

How many lemons do you have left in ending Inventory using FIFO? Fifty.

And how many lemons are left in ending Inventory using LIFO? Fifty.

We've got 50 lemons either way! With both FIFO and LIFO, you have exactly the same thing out on your lemonade stand. If you compare the FIFO and LIFO Balance Sheets, you have the same cash ($59), receivables ($11), 50 lemons, and a $2 insurance policy. So, by looking at our lemonade stand, could you tell what method of valuing Inventory we're using? No. No, it's just on paper.

LIFO and FIFO are ways of valuing inventory where? Just on paper.

Now, maybe you're thinking that LIFO would be a problem with a perishable product, like lemons. In other words, if you don't use the old lemons, what happens to them? They spoil.

Let's look at this situation. Here are two bowls of lemons.

The left bowl holds the lemons from our imaginary pipeline. In other words, the First-In lemons.

The right bowl holds the lemons from our imaginary barrel. In other words, the Last-In lemons.

On FIFO, which lemons will we use? The first-in lemons. At what cost? Twenty cents each.

On LIFO, which lemons will we use? The last-in lemons.

And what cost? Forty cents each. But now, think about this for a moment. If we actually use the last ones in, what will happen to the first (or old) lemons?

They'll spoil. Then rot. Then attract all sorts of disgusting mold and vermin. Then the health department will show up...you get the idea!

Which lemons should we use on LIFO? The first ones. At what cost (be careful here!)? Forty cents—remember the valuation is just on paper.

The point is, LIFO and FIFO are methods of valuing inventory. Are they methods of using inventory? No.

Which lemons will we always use? The first ones. Otherwise, they will spoil and rot.

LIFO is just creative accounting. You would always USE the older lemons first, but with LIFO you just PRETEND that you would use the new ones. Really, you are using the old lemons and the new price. As we learned earlier, this is just a creative way to save taxes.

You might be wondering if you can switch methods. The answer is yes and no.

Let me explain, starting with switching from FIFO to LIFO. Most companies start on the simpler method, FIFO. You can switch from FIFO to LIFO, the first time on your own. And why would you want to do that? In an inflationary economy, in which costs are going up, you would save on taxes. Once you have made that first switch, though, you cannot make a second switch without permission from the IRS. (The IRS?! And your were worried about the health inspector?)

It's rare that the IRS will grant permission for a business to make the second switch from LIFO back to FIFO. You must file for permission with the IRS Commissioner and that permission must be granted before you switch a second time.

If you switch from LIFO to FIFO, would you have to pay back the taxes that had been saved? Yes, I'm afraid so.

In reality, would the taxes ever catch up with you? To answer, let's look at when they could catch up with us.

On LIFO, what is the book value of our 50 lemons? $10.00.

But what would it cost us to buy 50 lemons now? $20.00.

So, suppose you sold the business. What would you sell the 50 lemons for? $20. Ah, so you would have $10 in earnings and owe what? Taxes!

Suppose we sold the last 50 lemons, then our ending inventory is what? Zero.

The taxes would catch up then. So, we can save the taxes due on the $10 difference as long as we always keep at least how many lemons? Fifty.

One last thing regarding FIFO versus LIFO. How would you know what method a company is using?

Well, there is a special section of a company's financials that's called footnotes.

In the footnotes, a company is required to reveal the method it uses to value its inventory. In the footnotes, a company can also disclose the difference between the FIFO and LIFO amounts, so that investors will know that assets are "understated" on LIFO. However, the government does not allow companies to show FIFO on financial statements and LIFO on tax reports. Unless a company wants to have some serious explaining to do, all external reporting has to be consistent.

Okay, but can you average the cost of inventory?

Yes. Many companies do use the average cost method. If your inventory can be specifically identified, like items with serial numbers, you can always value inventory by specific identification.

Before getting back to our lemonade business, let's summarize the FIFO versus LIFO methods.

FIFO and LIFO are ways to value inventory on what? Paper.

The only reason anyone would use LIFO is to save what? Taxes.

Phew! That's the end of another week. Time to give yourself a break before moving on. Put on some music and dance around. Go outside for some fresh air. Do some stretches.

Or, I know, pour yourself a refreshing glass of ice-cold lemonade!

CHAPTER 7

Like we do at the start of every new week, what's the first thing we do? Roll up the earnings from last week.

We're going to stick with LIFO, by the way, for the rest of the book because we want to save taxes.

NOTE: In real life, LIFO records are difficult and expensive to maintain. Only companies with large amounts of inventory would adopt this method. Consult a good accountant when making this decision.

Enough of the legal warnings and mumbo-jumbo—let's get rolling. Roll up the earnings from week three.

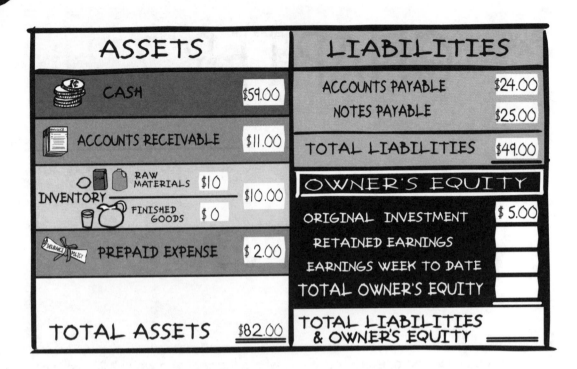

What's our Retained Earnings? Twenty-eight dollars. And, given the new week, week four, what's our Earnings Week to Date? None, so far.

First thing, though, you receive a phone call from one of your friends who bought some lemonade on account several weeks ago. He finally got his allowance and is ready to pay you five dollars. This is great! You collected on an account without having to call in the collection agency.

Did we receive Cash? Yes.

So what do we have to do to demonstrate this?

Add $5 in cash and take away $5 in Accounts Receivable. Use the next Balance Sheet to demonstrate this transaction.

ASSETS		LIABILITIES	
CASH		ACCOUNTS PAYABLE	$24.00
		NOTES PAYABLE	$25.00
ACCOUNTS RECEIVABLE		TOTAL LIABILITIES	$49.00
INVENTORY — RAW MATERIALS $10 / FINISHED GOODS $0	$10.00	**OWNER'S EQUITY**	
		ORIGINAL INVESTMENT	$5.00
PREPAID EXPENSE	$2.00	RETAINED EARNINGS	$28.00
		EARNINGS WEEK TO DATE	
		TOTAL OWNER'S EQUITY	$33.00
TOTAL ASSETS		TOTAL LIABILITIES & OWNER'S EQUITY	$82.00

Did we account for that Accounts Receivable as a sale a few weeks back? Yes.

Did it show up on our Income Statement as a sale back then? Yes.

Are we going to account for it as a sale now? No.

No, because we already accounted for it as a sale on our Income Statement when? Two weeks ago.

That's because we are using the Accrual Method of accounting.

Is any part of this transaction going to show up on your Income Statement? No.

But, we did get in some cash, didn't we? Would it be helpful to keep track of our cash as it flows in and out of the business? Yes.

We're going to bring out our third financial statement. Why three?

Think it of this way. At least, how many legs does a stool need to be stable? Three.

If we think of our financial record-keeping as a stool, the Balance Sheet is one leg. The Income Statement is another leg. So, we need another leg for our financial stool to become stable.

And we've been managing our business with an income statement and a balance sheet. Both of which are on what method? The Accrual Method.

The third financial statement is the Cash Flow Statement.

Here's a Cash Statement. We're going to build it line by line.

CASH STATEMENT WEEK _____		
COLLECTIONS	$	
INVENTORY PAID		
FIXED ASSET INVESTMENT		
EXPENSES PAID		
CHANGE IN CASH		$
BEGINNING CASH		+
ENDING CASH		$

We're going to go through it line by line and, at the end of the week, we'll put the whole Cash Statement together.

Basically, the Cash Statement records only the cash that comes in and the cash that goes out in a given time period—in our case, each week. This bears repeating:

The Cash Statement records only the cash that comes in and the cash that goes out.

Did we start this week with some cash? Yes.

How much was the beginning cash? $59.00. Record that on the Beginning Cash line.

Now, did we collect five dollars on our account? Yes.

Record the cash that comes in and the cash that goes out. We'll put in a plus if cash comes in and a minus if cash goes out. On what line of our Cash Statement would this $5 go? Well, it was a collection, right? So add plus $5 to Collections.

You can write A/R next to the $5 so you will know it was from collecting Accounts Receivable. Got that?

The Change in Cash line is where you will total all the pluses and minuses at the end of the week, based on all the detail line items above.

Given that you're such an entrepreneur—and once an entrepreneur, always an entrepreneur—you decide to spruce up your place of business. A friend's older brother has a great stand that he built a couple years ago when he had his own lemonade business. You decide to buy it. You negotiate a hard deal and get the stand for eight dollars.

Another friend's family has a tiny patch of land they're willing to sell you for your new location. It's part of an enormous vacant lot that, while locating near the corner of a busy street, is years away from serious development.

You buy the lot and the new lemonade stand for $10 cash.

You expect the stand will last about 10 years without major repairs. In the initial sales contract, you specify that $8 of the purchase is for the stand and $2 is for the land.

(There is a reason for separating these which we'll discuss later.)

How do we demonstrate that on our Balance Sheet? We're going to put our brand new stand in a corner lot for $10.

What are we going to buy it with? Cash.

Okay. Ten dollars goes out. What comes in? The new stand and lot.

Is the stand and lot something we have? Yes.

So, where are we going to show it? Is it an Asset? Yes.

What are we going to call it? What does a business call something it has acquired which is property, plant, or equipment? A Fixed Asset. Why "fixed"? Because it's things not normally intended for sale, which are used over and over again in the course of doing business.

Go ahead and do another Balance Sheet, reflecting this transaction.

ASSETS			LIABILITIES	
CASH			ACCOUNTS PAYABLE	$24.00
			NOTES PAYABLE	$25.00
ACCOUNTS RECEIVABLE	$6.00		TOTAL LIABILITIES	$49.00
INVENTORY — RAW MATERIALS $10 / FINISHED GOODS $0		$10.00	**OWNER'S EQUITY**	
			ORIGINAL INVESTMENT	$5.00
PREPAID EXPENSE	$2.00		RETAINED EARNINGS	$28.00
			EARNINGS WEEK TO DATE	
FIXED ASSETS			TOTAL OWNER'S EQUITY	$33.00
TOTAL ASSETS			**TOTAL LIABILITIES & OWNER'S EQUITY**	$82.00

Besides a building or land, what other Fixed Assets can you think of?

_____

_____

_____

Maybe you wrote down things like office furniture, business vehicles, computers, tools, fax machines, telephones, book shelves, refrigerator—things like that.

We just bought a Fixed Asset. Is it ours? Yes. How much? $10.00.

Do you know what it's called when you buy an asset and add it to the Balance Sheet? Capitalizing the asset.

Now, does the purchase of the land or the stand show up on your Income Statement? No.

Can we take the stand and the land as an expense? No.

How come we can't expense them? Because it is a major purchase of significant value with a long life.

What's the rule here? Generally, the purchase of major items of significant value increase your assets and are added to the Balance Sheet, that is, capitalized.

One more time?

Generally, the purchase of major items of significant value increase your assets and are added to the Balance Sheet (capitalized).

Deciding whether to capitalize or expense an item is a pretty important decision that has some general guidelines. We will look at a few examples, then clarify the guidelines.

We've just transferred cash into another kind of asset, and capitalized the asset. Do you see it?

Did cash go out? Yes.

We made a what? An investment.

Go back to your Cash Statement and put minus $10 on the Cash Statement, on which line? Fixed Asset Investment.

You like the new lemonade stand, but your friend's older brother didn't have great taste in paint. (Unless you call brown, purple, and hot pink an appealing combination.) The stand needs a paint job—and fast! It's present condition won't exactly attract many customers, so you decide to paint it yourself in bright colors.

You know that the local hardware store often has odds and ends in its paint department that are priced way down. You call and, sure enough, you can get a couple cans of paint for two dollars.

The paint dealer is a bit odd. He works at a hardware store, but he wears a French beret, a long white smock, and will only answer to the name, "Monsieur Claude." You say, "Bon jour, Monsieur Claude. Here's $2 for two cans. Merci!" One can is bright yellow. The other is a pretty shade of blue.

You go back and paint your stand. To your eyes, it's a masterpiece. Right up there with the Mona Lisa!

How are we going to account for this paint?

Did cash go out? Yep, you put that $2 in paint all over the stand.

On which of our three financial statements do we record this transaction? We'll get to this in a few moments.

Before we do, let's stop and consider whether we should take the paint as an improvement and capitalize it—or expense it.

Do we want to add the paint to the Fixed Assets and, as a result, capitalize it? Does it increase the value of the stand?

Do we expense it?

Do you think we could do either?

Well, in fact, you could do either. If it is Super-Sticky, Weather-Bester Paint and lasts 10 years, we would do what? Capitalize it.

Suppose it's the cheap stuff that peels the first year. What should we do? Expense it. Say, it's the cheap stuff—would you have to paint that stand every year? Yes. Would that be an on-going cost of doing business? Yes. A maintenance expense? Yes.

Guess which paint we got for our hard-earned money? The cheap stuff.

Okay, then. We take it as an expense which means we're going to have to do what? Reduce earnings.

Complete a new Balance Sheet that reflects the expensing of the paint.

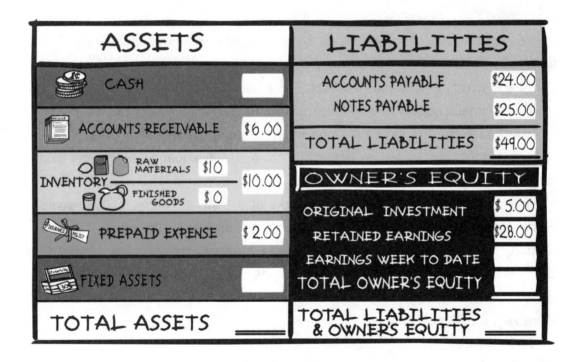

This might throw you into an interesting dilemma when you go to reduce earnings by $2. How much do you have in Earnings Week to Date? ZERO, ZIP, ZILCH! You could be tempted to subtract $2 from Retained Earnings—but those are past earnings and we do not want to change the past. In accounting, you are always working in the present or current accounting period. That means our earnings in this period are now minus $2. This is what is commonly referred to in business as being in the "red." You might want to get a red marker to write this in, or put the amount in brackets to signify the loss.

How did this happen? How did such a thriving, promising, expanding lemonade business suddenly plunge into the "red"? The explanation is simple. You've been so busy making improvements, buying fixed assets, scheming and dreaming, etc.—that you haven't opened for business this week!

For the Earnings Week to Date, we're in the red! And by how much? $2.00.

Did we pay cash for the paint? Does it also show up on the Cash Statement we started earlier in this chapter? Yes.

Did cash come in or go out? Out.

Cash for the paint went out. It's minus 2 in expenses paid on our Cash Statement. Go back and write that in.

Let's review. All three financial statements get used in this transaction.

On the Balance Sheet, cash goes out and we expense it, which reduces earnings. It gets recorded on our Income Statement as paint expense for $2. And it also gets recorded on the Cash Statement as minus $2 under expenses paid. Okay?

Gee, the new lemonade stand looks great. It's really solid and the shingle roof adds character. The color scheme is great, too. Which makes you wish you could add one more thing before really, really starting to sell some lemonade this week. It would make your life so much easier if you just had a sink. With a sink you could wash and re-use glasses on the spot, instead of having to cart them home every night.

You make a few calls. New sinks are very expensive. But you find a place that sells used stuff that has a decent sink for only $2. Better still, because the owner doesn't live that far away, he'll deliver the sink for free on his way home! And, even better still, the owner is happy to let you charge the sink.

The owner brings the sink over, as promised, and stays to help you hitch it on to your lemonade stand.

How do we demonstrate this transaction? Accounts Payable goes up.

By how much? $2.00.

Will we have to replace the sink every year? No. Does it improve the stand? Yes. Being an improvement, how do we account for it? Capitalize it.

So, do we want to set up another Fixed Asset for the sink? No.

What will we do? Add it to the stand.

We're going to hitch that sink right on to our stand, aren't we? With a little help. yes.

Are we increasing the value of our stand? Yes.

By how much? $2.00.

Demonstrate these transaction on the next Balance Sheet.

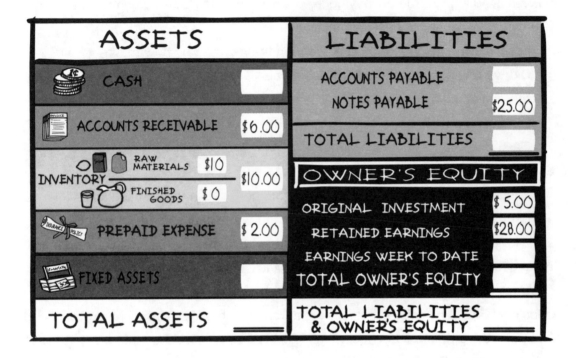

ASSETS		LIABILITIES	
CASH		ACCOUNTS PAYABLE	
		NOTES PAYABLE	$25.00
ACCOUNTS RECEIVABLE	$6.00	TOTAL LIABILITIES	
INVENTORY — RAW MATERIALS $10 / FINISHED GOODS $0	$10.00	OWNER'S EQUITY	
		ORIGINAL INVESTMENT	$5.00
PREPAID EXPENSE	$2.00	RETAINED EARNINGS	$28.00
		EARNINGS WEEK TO DATE	
FIXED ASSETS		TOTAL OWNER'S EQUITY	
TOTAL ASSETS	___	TOTAL LIABILITIES & OWNER'S EQUITY	___

But wait a minute! Why are we not expensing the sink? We expensed the paint.

Here's why. We said that we'll be buying paint every year as an on-going cost of doing business. So it has a short life. But the sink will last for years.

If we were to sell that stand, would the sink increase the value of our stand? Yes.

If you add something that improves an asset, you capitalize it. So, if we increase the value of the stand we are making a capital improvement.

Did cash get affected by buying the sink? No.

Why? We charged it.

Does it show up on the Cash Statement? No.

Since we capitalized the asset, does that show up as an expense on the Income Statement? No.

This transaction only shows up where? In which financial statement? The Balance Sheet.

You're so busy, fixing the stand and climbing all over it that you crack a roof shingle. You want the stand to look perfect and figure it shouldn't cost too much to replace a single shingle. You ask your friend's brother and he says he'll repair it for one dollar. He even allows you to charge it.

Is the repair an expense? Yes.

For how much? $1.00.

Did you pay cash for it? No.

You charged it, right?

How do we demonstrate it?

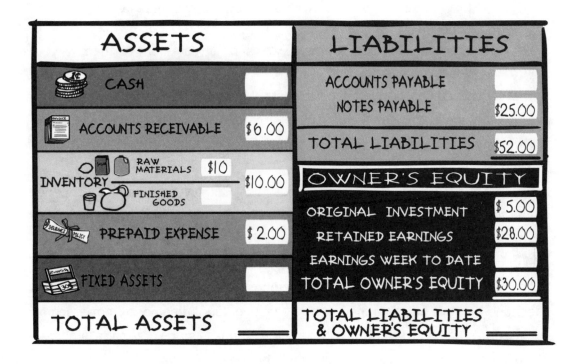

Add $1 to Accounts Payable and go in the red by another $1.00.

Did we stay in balance? Yes.

So, did this transaction only affect the right side of the Balance Sheet? Yes.

Is that okay? Yes. As long as both sides still balance.

What would make the roof repair a capital improvement? You'd have to add a whole new roof.

Did we just return the roof to the way it originally was? Yes.

So, is this another on-going cost of doing business? Yes.

A maintenance expense? Yes.

Does this show up on our Income Statement? Yes.

Did cash go out? No.

Since no cash went out, was the Cash Statement affected in any way? No.

The last four transactions involved the decision to capitalize or expense an item. Let's take the time now to review.

How does a business decide whether to expense or capitalize an item? There are two main criteria for the decision. What are they?

> 1. Time. How long the item lasts. You capitalize something that lasts longer than one year. Conversely, if it lasts less than a year you would expense it.
> 2. Cost. If you buy a trash can and it lasts longer than a year, would you capitalize it? No. Why not? It's too insignificant of an item.

The second criteria is how much it costs. Most companies have a set dollar amount. What are examples? $500, $1000, $1500. So, let's pick $500—if your company's policy is $500 and the item is less than $500 we automatically expense it. If it is $500 and above we capitalize it.

Well, it's finally, *finally* time to open for business. But, given all that has happened and the time it has taken, you forget to make time to buy some lemons and sugar and make more lemonade.

Oh, my gosh! Now what?!

Although it stands for everything you oppose, and you hope your customers understand that this one time they won't be tasting your homemade-from-a-secret-recipe, world's-greatest-tasting lemonade—you purchase some pre-made lemonade for $20 in cash. The carton says it contains a hundred glasses.

What do you think of this—is it a good idea? No.

Why not? Freshness and uniqueness of product are going down.

But check this out. What kind of pre-made is it? Truman's Own.

Will the kids buy it? You bet!

How did we pay for it? Cash.

How much cash? $20.00.

Let's demonstrate on the Balance Sheet.

ASSETS		LIABILITIES	
CASH		ACCOUNTS PAYABLE	$27.00
		NOTES PAYABLE	$25.00
ACCOUNTS RECEIVABLE		TOTAL LIABILITIES	$52.00
INVENTORY — RAW MATERIALS $10		OWNER'S EQUITY	
FINISHED GOODS		ORIGINAL INVESTMENT	$ 5.00
PREPAID EXPENSE	$ 2.00	RETAINED EARNINGS	$28.00
		EARNINGS WEEK TO DATE	
FIXED ASSETS	$12.00	TOTAL OWNER'S EQUITY	
TOTAL ASSETS		TOTAL LIABILITIES & OWNER'S EQUITY	

Are we in balance? Yes.

Did cash go out? Yes.

What we did was make a cash purchase. Record that on your Cash Statement under Inventory Period. To make life easier, here's a fresh Cash Statement below. Transfer all of the previous cash transactions in this chapter. Then, record the purchase of the pre-made lemonade. What happened? Cash went down by $20.00.

CASH STATEMENT WEEK _____

COLLECTIONS	$
INVENTORY PAID	
FIXED ASSET INVESTMENT	
EXPENSES PAID	
CHANGE IN CASH	$
BEGINNING CASH	+
ENDING CASH	$

Does the purchase of pre-made lemonade show up on our Income Statement? *Yes, under the purchases section of Cost of Goods Sold for $20.00.*

So, we've got this pre-made lemonade and guess what? Sales are great! You sell all the pre-made lemonade for $50. Forty dollars in cash and $10 on account. Other inventory remains the same.

What goes out? *Lemonade.*

We've still got the old lemons. Although they're starting to look a little, well…old.

What comes in? *Cash.*

How much cash? *$40.00.*

And how much on account? *$10.00.*

Update the left side of the Balance Sheet.

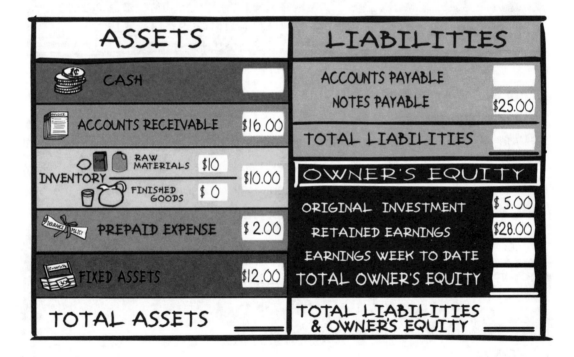

Are we in balance? *Not yet.*

So, we need to reflect what? *Earnings week to date.*

Our sales were $50—and how much did it cost us in Inventory? *$20.00.*

So, what are total earnings this week? *$30.00.*

But what are the earnings on the Balance Sheet, before reflecting the day's sales? *Minus $3.00.*

So $30 minus $3 equals how much? $27.00.

Okay, update the right side of the Balance Sheet above.

Now, are we in balance? Yes.

Now, let's go back for a minute to the last Cash Statement on the previous page.

Did cash get affected? Yes.

We collected $40. Record +40 on the Collections line.

Now that we finally had some sales—and, more importantly, some cash came in, we want to keep our good relationship with Pappy Parker, our grocer. Our original account with the kind old gent is almost 30 days—or close to overdue. So, we decide to pay $4.00 on our account for sugar.

We get on our bike and go down to the grocery store. "How's the lemonade business?" Pappy asks. If he's worried about getting paid he's not showing it.

"Today, things are definitely looking up," you say. "So I want to pay you $4.00, in cash."

Pappy happily takes four dollars. In return, he gives you a free cookie. Doing business with some people is such fun!

Okay, you pay the grocer with what? Cash.

So, what comes out? Cash, for $4.00.

Do the Balance Sheet below.

ASSETS		LIABILITIES	
CASH		ACCOUNTS PAYABLE	
		NOTES PAYABLE	$25.00
ACCOUNTS RECEIVABLE	$16.00	TOTAL LIABILITIES	
INVENTORY — RAW MATERIALS $10 / FINISHED GOODS $0	$10.00	**OWNER'S EQUITY**	
		ORIGINAL INVESTMENT	$5.00
PREPAID EXPENSE	$2.00	RETAINED EARNINGS	$28.00
		EARNINGS WEEK TO DATE	$27.00
FIXED ASSETS	$12.00	TOTAL OWNER'S EQUITY	$60.00
TOTAL ASSETS	___	**TOTAL LIABILITIES & OWNER'S EQUITY**	___

What gets reduced on the right side, to be balanced? Accounts Payable, BY $4.00.

Now that $4 for sugar—has that shown up on our Income Statement before? Yes.

Will it show up on the Income Statement this week? No.

When did we account for that as a purchase? When it happened in Week 2.

Right, on the Accrual Method we accounted for it then even though we didn't pay any what? Cash.

Here it is, two weeks later and we're paying back in what? Cash.

Do the Accounts Payable show up as part of cost of goods sold this week on our Income Statement? No.

Nothing happens on the Income Statement.

But did cash get affected? Yes.

Cash goes down by how much? $4.00.

We'll put a minus 4 right by Inventory Paid—and note that we paid Pappy the grocer back. Please update the Cash Statement on page 109.

Having paid Pappy some, you figure why not spread your good fortune around. You decide to pay back the bank $25 for loan, plus $2 for interest. The banker happily takes $27 from you. On the way out, the bank guard smiles at you and says, "Come back again soon. Hear?"

How much goes out? $27.00. Right, $25 on the principal—and $2 in what? Interest.

So, how much Cash goes out? $27.00.

Show this transaction on the next Balance Sheet.

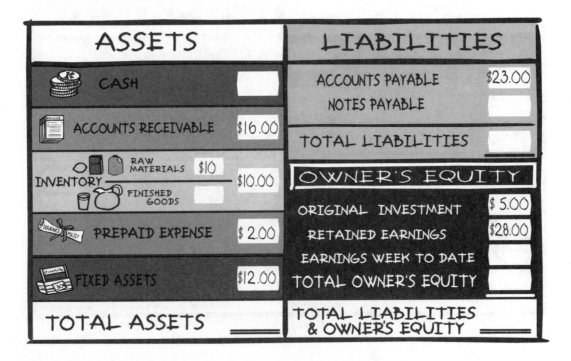

ASSETS		LIABILITIES	
CASH		ACCOUNTS PAYABLE	$23.00
		NOTES PAYABLE	
ACCOUNTS RECEIVABLE	$16.00	TOTAL LIABILITIES	
INVENTORY — RAW MATERIALS $10 / FINISHED GOODS	$10.00	OWNER'S EQUITY	
		ORIGINAL INVESTMENT	$5.00
PREPAID EXPENSE	$2.00	RETAINED EARNINGS	$28.00
		EARNINGS WEEK TO DATE	
FIXED ASSETS	$12.00	TOTAL OWNER'S EQUITY	
TOTAL ASSETS		TOTAL LIABILITIES & OWNER'S EQUITY	

Are we in balance yet? *No.*

What do we need to do on the right side? We need to take off what? *Notes Payable by $25.* Are we in balance now? *Not yet.*

We also need to account for paying the interest expense, on the right side. So, what comes out of earnings? *$2.00.*

Now, complete the right side of the Balance Sheet.

Are you in balance now? *Yes. The totals should be $81.00.*

That $2 is an interest expense. Our cost of doing business with the bank.

Does any of the transaction regarding the loan pay back show up on the Income Statement? *Yes, interest.*

Interest expense for how much? *$2.00*

Is the Cash Statement affected? *Yes, because cash went out.*

Now, $27 went out. We didn't borrow, but we paid back the bank $25 for what? *The principal.*

So, on the next Cash Statement, record the pay back—$25 of the principal on borrow/payback (Bring forward the numbers from page 109.)

In addition, put minus $2 on the Expenses Paid line.

CASH STATEMENT WEEK _____

COLLECTIONS	$	
INVENTORY PAID		
FIXED ASSET INVESTMENT		
EXPENSES PAID		
CHANGE IN CASH	$	
BEGINNING CASH	+	
ENDING CASH	$	

Okay. We want to introduce one more thing before closing out this week. It's how to treat the value of fixed assets over time. This concept is called "depreciation." What is depreciation? It's the decrease in value of fixed assets over time due to wear and tear and obsolescence.

Let's look at our major fixed assets, the stand, the lot it sits on, and the sink we added to the stand.

We bought the stand for $8 and the land for $2.

What did we add to the stand that was capitalized? The sink.

The building and sink are now $10 and the land is $2.

Why separate the land? By law, you can't depreciate land.

Why not? Give some reasons why you think we can't depreciate land.

_____

_____

_____

How long does land last? Forever. (Except in California, right?)

Does land wear out? No.

Therefore, can we depreciate land? No.

But, can we depreciate the stand? Yes.

And the sink? Yes.

Can we depreciate the stand and improvement? Yes.

How long did we say the stand is going to last? Ten years.

And we can depreciate how much? $10.00.

The method of depreciation we're going to use is called Straight Line Depreciation. The way that straight line depreciation works is that you draw a straight line between the number of years (10 years) and the dollar amount...what did it cost you? $10.00.

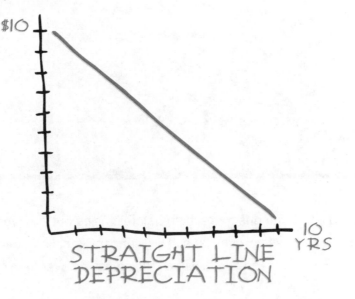

STRAIGHT LINE DEPRECIATION

Using straight line depreciation, each year represents an equal percentage, how much is each year worth of the total depreciation? *10 percent if it is a ten-year life.*

Therefore, if the total amount we can depreciate is $10 and the length of time is ten years, we can take $1 per year. If we take $1 for the first few years, it's going to lower the value of our fixed asset by that amount. Which means that our $12.00 fixed asset is now worth $11.00.

Does that mean it's really worth $11? *No.*

It's now worth $11 on paper. That's called the net book value. When you hear the net book value of a fixed asset, it means purchase price minus depreciation. We will show this on our Balance Sheet using **red** (negative) for the depreciation.

On paper, the value is going down. In reality, though, out in the world, the value might be going up.

Now, on our Balance Sheet, if we reduce the value of the fixed asset by one dollar, are we in balance? *No.*

What is depreciation? *An expense.* And expenses reduce what? *Earnings.*

So what do you have to do here? *Reduce earnings by $1.00.*

Show the depreciation transactions on the next Balance Sheet.

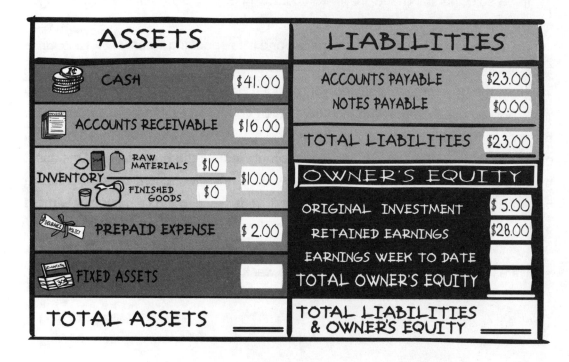

Did depreciation affect our Cash? *No.* Right, it's the first time we've had an expense that didn't affect our Cash position at all.

But, we get to take it as a what? *An expense.*

Turning to our Income Statement, where would we write this down? *As Depreciation Expense.*

Now, here's another accounting rule for us to lock into our memory forever:

Remember: Depreciation is a non-cash expense.

Like our other rules, this bears repeating.

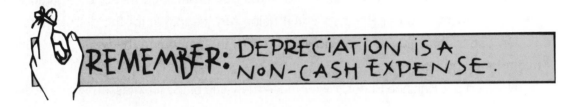

This is different from the insurance policy. When we took the prepaid expenses for the first year's insurance we used up $1. Could we get the whole $3 back for it? *No.*

If we sold the stand and the sink, could we get $10 back for it? *Maybe. Maybe even more.*

So depreciation is a non-cash expense and it's happening where? *On the Balance Sheet, on PAPER.*

Now, the government is saying you paid $10 for the sink and the stand, but we won't let you expense the whole amount when you buy it; you have to capitalize it. But it's going to start wearing out, in theory. So, we'll let you take $1 as a non-cash expense. As a result, each year we would simply reduce the book value of the asset by the depreciation amount which obviously does not affect cash. This is why it is a non-cash expense. The advantage is that it reduces earnings and taxes without reducing cash. *(Pretty nifty, huh?)*

Here is your final Balance Sheet for this week. Please complete it.

ENDING BALANCE SHEET FOR WEEK FOUR

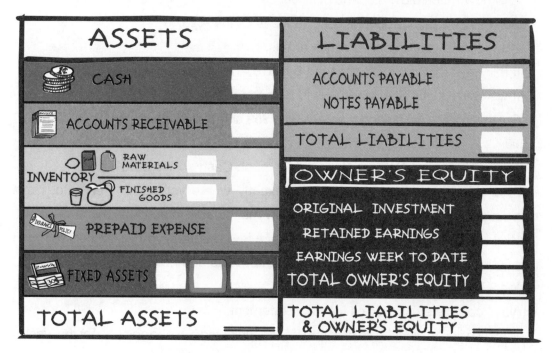

Now, complete the cash statement below.

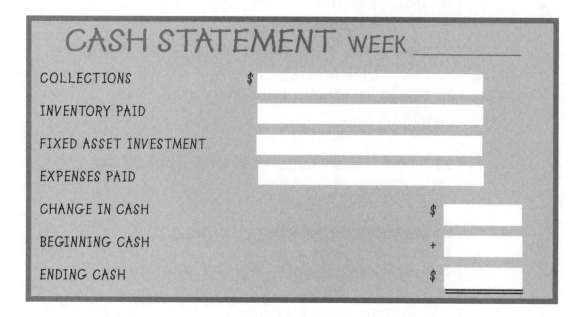

How much did we collect? $45.00.

And how much did we spend? $63.00.

So, +$45 and -$63. What is the change is cash? -$18.00

Now, before you go on, let's look at this.

If this says that our cash changed by -$18, then it went down by $18.

If we started with $59, what should be our ending cash? $41.00

So, that means we started the week with $59 and ended the week with how much? $41.00.

Look on your last Balance Sheet. How much Cash do we have? $41.00.

And, this Cash Statement tells you exactly where your cash went. So, it's a recording of your cash transactions and how much came in and how much went out.

Wow! You're doing great! In the matter of a few chapters, you've learned so much accounting—including the three financial statements and how to use them!

Well done!

Now, complete this week's Income Statement.

Because you're working so hard and having fun doing it, we're going to list the week's transactions, so you don't have to go back and find every last one. *You're welcome!*

TRANSACTIONS:

You collect $5 cash from some of your friends.

You buy a lot and a new lemonade stand for $10 cash.

You pay $2 cash for paint and apply it to the stand.

You buy a sink for $2 and charge it.

You repair the roof for $1 and charge it.

You pay $20 cash for pre-made lemonade.

Sales are good. You sell all the pre-made lemonade for $50—$40 cash and $10 on Account.

You pay back your accounts payable for sugar for $4.

You pay back the loan for $25 plus $2 in interest.

You depreciate the building and improvements ($10 total) using straight line depreciation. Show this year's depreciation expense for $1.

Ph-eww! What a week! While I catch my breath, go ahead and complete this week's Income Statement.

INCOME STATEMENT   Begin: Monday A.M. End: Sunday P.M.
SALES $ ____

    Beginning Inventory $ ____
    + Purchases
    + Labor
    Total Available for Sale $ ____
    - Ending Inventory
= COST OF GOODS SOLD   ____
GROSS PROFIT =   ____
EXPENSES
    • _____   ____
    • _____   ____
= TOTAL EXPENSES   ____
NET PROFIT (Gross Profit - Expenses) $ ____

Let's check the Income Statement.

Sales were $50.

Beginning Inventory was $10.

Purchases were $20.

So, Total Available for Sale was $30.

The Ending Inventory was $10.

Which means the Cost of Goods Sold was $20.

Leaving you with a Gross Profit of $30.

The Expenses were: Paint, $2; roof repair, $1; Interest, $2; Depreciation, $1. For a Total Expenses of $6.

Leaving you with a Net Profit of...drum roll please...$24!

Well, that completes another week. Next, we round third base and head for home!

CHAPTER 8

T he summer is moving right along. August is approaching, when your family takes its annual vacation. There's only a week or two before the vacation, and after that school starts. Which means you only have a brief time left to operate your lemonade stand and learn more about accounting.

It's Monday, and you're about to start a new week: week five. What's the first thing you do? Roll up the earnings from the last week.

Go ahead and do that.

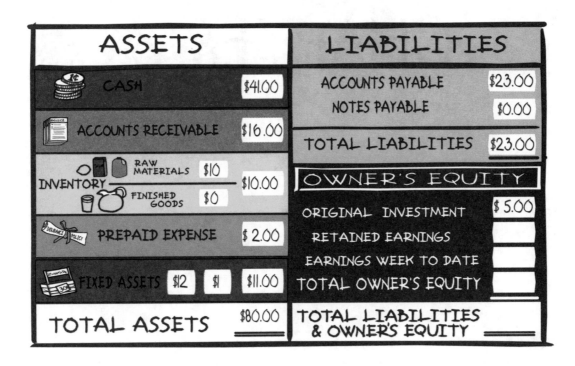

Okay, with last week now officially behind us, it's time to tackle a new week's challenges.

The first challenge isn't long in coming. Business is slow and, at first, you can't figure out why. The weather's nice and warm. Certainly everyone seems to like your new stand. No one seems to have minded that your lemonade is no longer made from scratch. What gives?

A friend rides by on her bike. You yell at her to stop for some lemonade. She yells back, "I can't right now. My sister's playing in the all-city softball tournament at the park. If I don't get there early I won't find a seat—because everyone's going to be there!"

Ah-ha!

A lot of potential customers are gathered at the softball fields at the park. But your stand is nailed to the ground here! If only you could find a way to get your great-tasting lemonade to this mass of customers....

Ah-ha!

You should get a mobile lemonade stand! One you can take to where crowds are. Because if you can't get your customers to come to where your business is located, then a smart businessperson goes to where the customers are!

You look in the phone book and make a lot of calls. Finally, you find a company which sells mobile refreshment stands, but they're thousands of dollars! Well, there's no way you can afford one of those, so it's time to get creative.

Let's see. You're not old enough to have a driver's license, so you don't need anything with a motor. You don't own a horse or mule, so you'll likely have to pull this unit by yourself. It doesn't have to be that big, you know—just big enough to carry your supplies. And it can't cost too much.

Hmmmm.

Then it hits you like a bolt from the blue! A wagon! Like the one you saw in the hardware store when you were there buying paint. Yes!

You get Dad to drive you to the hardware store.

The lady who sells wagons is Monsieur Claude's twin sister. She wears a red-checked flannel shirt, red suspenders, and tucks her wool pants into tall black boots. She has her long, gray hair in a ponytail tied with a red rubberband. Her name tag reads, "Wonderful Willa Wagner."

"I'm interested in buying a wagon," you tell her. "How much are they?"

"We happen to be running a special on our very best model," she tells you. "It's built of the highest grade steel. Its paint is rust-resistant. The tires are puncture-proof. A wonderful example of old-world craftsmanship. It has an estimated life of ten years, and the cost is a mere $20."

This woman obviously knows her wagons! You immediately decide you want it, you need it—you buy it!

Let's demonstrate the purchase on the Balance Sheet.

Do we have enough Cash to pay for it? *Yes. You take $20 from Cash to buy the mobile unit.*

Is the wagon another Asset? *Yes.*

What kind of Asset? *Fixed Asset.*

How much is it? *$20.00.*

But do we want to simply throw the wagon in with our other fixed assets—the stand, lot, and sink? *No.* Why not? *Well...because...ah...help me!*

Let's look at our other Fixed Assets, starting with our lemonade stand. Is it attached to the land? Yes. It's like a building, right? Right.

What about this wagon? Is it attached to the land? No, it's mobile.

Is the wagon like a building or plant? No.

A Fixed Asset that's movable is called what? Equipment.

A-ha! There are different types of Fixed Assets.

Many companies separate equipment from buildings on the Balance Sheet.

Now, because the wagon is equipment, is that the only reason it's set up as a separate fixed asset on the Balance Sheet? No. Can you think of another reason why?

_____

_____

Well, another reason is, since it's a different type of Fixed Asset, we can depreciate it differently.

Let's do the next Balance Sheet, reflecting the wagon purchase.

ASSETS				LIABILITIES	
CASH				ACCOUNTS PAYABLE	$23.00
				NOTES PAYABLE	$ 0.00
ACCOUNTS RECEIVABLE		$16.00		TOTAL LIABILITIES	$23.00
INVENTORY — RAW MATERIALS	$10	$10.00		**OWNER'S EQUITY**	
FINISHED GOODS	$ 0			ORIGINAL INVESTMENT	$ 5.00
PREPAID EXPENSE		$ 2.00		RETAINED EARNINGS	$52.00
FIXED ASSETS	$12 $1	$11.00		EARNINGS WEEK TO DATE	$ 0.00
FIXED ASSETS				TOTAL OWNER'S EQUITY	$57.00
TOTAL ASSETS		____		**TOTAL LIABILITIES & OWNER'S EQUITY**	$80.00

It's very late on Saturday afternoon when you start for the softball tournament. Not to worry—it's an evening tournament and the first game gets underway in fifteen minutes.

You head out across the neighborhood to the game, feeling on top of the world. After all, you've just bought that shining red wagon and you're going to the game to cash in on another great entrepreneurial idea.

On the way, you go by Pappy's grocery store to buy more Truman's Own. But the store is closed! You don't know what's going on—then you remember Mr. Parker said he was closing early today so he could go to the game. You're a little worried about Pappy's store being closed because you need more inventory.

You decide to push on. Hey, there's bound to be a store near the ball park.

Sure enough, a mere block from the field you see that you're in luck! There is a store and it's open. But, once inside, you realize it's one of the warehouse type stores that sells only in bulk. You look at the price and you really feel sick. Because the price here is $30—ten dollars more than what you paid at Pappy's for the same quantity.

Thirty dollars! Your heart sinks. What are you going to do? Because you only have $21 in the cigar box you brought along (Note cash on your last balance sheet.)

Looks like we have a major, MAJOR problem. What are we going to do? What would you do?

_____

_____

_____

What can we do? Go to Mom and Dad! Isn't that what parents are for? It's a good idea, but then you remember that Mom's at her weekly aerobics class and Dad took the afternoon to hit some golf balls at the driving range. No way can you reach them!

Now what?

Go to the bank and borrow some money. Is the bank open Saturday afternoons? No, It closes at noon on Saturday.

Maybe you could float a check! OHHH! Would our banker like that? No, and neither would the police!

You're desperate. This is the worst business situation since Coke tried to pull its old formula with a "new, improved" Coke! Since Ford rolled out the Edsel! Dang! You have this shiny, new mobile unit—but no lemonade to sell! What should you do?!

Sell the mobile unit!

The game's getting going any minute now. Are you going to have the time to sell the mobile unit and run to some other store for pre-made lemonade? No.

Besides, you need a place to put your lemonade.

What else might you do?

Put the squeeze on your friends who still owe you money! The Accounts Receivable.

Maybe. But none of them are at the game.

Can you return the wagon and get your money back? No Willa Wagner is at the tournament, like everyone else.

You could always buy less lemonade, right?

Sure, if you had all night to find a store that was opened and sold the brand you wanted.

Okay, you decide, I'll go to the insurance agent and get back your money on the policy.

But his office is closed, too.

Desperate people try desperate measures. It's not a proud moment…it's not something you'll tell your grandkids sixty years from now. You decide to use the old inventory.

But, for how long has it been hanging around? Weeks and weeks by now. So, can we use it? Only if we want a visit from the health inspector and a possible lawsuit on our hands.

Okay, what do a lot of start-up businesses do? Sell stock and go public.

At a softball tournament? These ideas have gone from bad to worse! Is there nothing we can try?

Finally, you ask some friends for advice. One of them says, "You've been bragging about all those retained earnings you've been rolling up all summer. Why don't you just spend some of those?"

Ah, a true friend!

Let's try this one, you decide.

You rush back to the store and say to the first clerk you see, "I want to buy some Truman's Own, pre-made lemonade."

"Yes, we carry it," the clerk says.

You are so happy and relieved that they have it that you feel like standing on your tiptoes and hugging the clerk.

"How much is it?" you ask, hoping you misread the high price.

"Thirty dollars," the clerk says. "We only sell it by the shrink-wrapped case."

"Cool. I'll take it," you say.

"How will you pay?" the clerk then asks.

"Well, I would like to give you $21 in cash and $9 of my retained earnings."

"Sorry," the clerk says. "Cash only."

You lay out the $21 dollars.

"That's not enough," the clerk says. "Where's the rest?"

"I have $9 in retained earnings. My earnings are as good as cash!" you insist.

"What we take here is green—the real stuff," the clerk says. "I see $21 in green. Are your earnings green?"

"Well, not exactly. They're black—as in 'in the black!'" you admit. "But won't you take my retained earnings? Please. PLEASE! Please, please, please, with whipped cream and a cherry on top! People have always told me I could spend my earnings. The only difference is my cash is green and my earnings are black."

"Sorry, no," the clerk says. With that, he smiles, shrugs, and walks away.

So, can you spend earnings? *No. You cannot spend earnings.* You can only spend what? *Cash.*

You're more than a little bewildered by this experience. Well, you think, if I can't spend my earnings, what good are they? And, by the way, if they aren't cash, where are they? You resolve to figure that out later.

Meanwhile, you're desperate! You're only a few dollars short and no one will help you! Maybe you should steal the lemonade. Wow, steal it? Do we want to do that? *I don't think so.*

Hey, Pappy Parker let you open an account. Maybe this nice looking clerk at the warehouse-type store will let you charge the lemonade.

You chase after him. You find him dusting shrink-wrapped cartons of toothpicks.

"Okay," you say, with as much confidence as you can muster. "I'd like to give you $21 cash and charge the balance. Will you do it?"

"I don't know you, kid," the clerk replies. "How do I know you will pay it back?"

"How about calling my personal grocer, Pappy Parker, across town? I've got credit with him and I've paid all my bills." Then you remember, again, that Pappy's at the tournament, like everyone else.

You beg with the clerk; you plead. You offer to leave your valuable polished rock that you always carry in your pocket for luck.

Finally, the clerk agrees to talk to the manager on your behalf. And, miracle of miracles, the manager agrees to let you open an account. He said something about knowing Pappy and that anyone who could get credit from Pappy is probably okay.

We give the clerk how much cash? $21.00

The clerk gives us how much lemonade? $30.00

Go ahead and demonstrate the transaction.

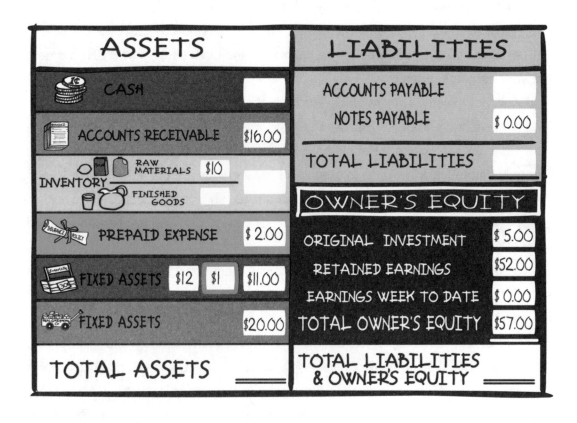

How do we balance it? Add $9.00 to Accounts Payable.

Are we in balance? Yes.

Let's take a moment to look at our Balance Sheet.

If someone showed you this Balance Sheet, what would you say about this business? Are we profitable? Do we have lots of assets? Pretty good for four weeks in the business.

Is there a problem? You bet there is!

What about our cash position? Don't ask!

Come on, what is the problem? No cash!

If we have rain and everybody goes home and doesn't buy any lemonade, what's going to happen? No cash coming from sales.

We have lots of assets. We just don't have lots of what? Cash. To be blunt, we have zero cash. Zip! Zilch! A big fat goose egg!

But our Balance Sheet says we have plenty of Retained Earnings. Aren't they cash? Don't we have them in the bank? We've been rolling up those earnings? Aren't they in an account?

That question is worth the whole summer's business.

You've probably heard people say, "I'm going to go spend my earnings." But what did we just discover? Merchants will not take earnings. You can only spend cash.

If earnings are not cash, where are your retained earnings? Certainly not available as cash.

So, right now, those earnings are tied up where? In assets, inventory, equipment.

Now, don't forget because this is worth the whole summer:

Earnings Are Not Cash!

Remember, the left side of our scorecard is a reflection of what's out at our stand. What we have in Cash, Inventory, etc. Look at the line items on the Balance Sheet. Find the line which represents our stand and sink. Our wagon. Our rotten lemons. Our insurance policy. The Receivables from friends.

And, the right side is a record on paper of who owns or who provided this stuff. The truth is, everything on the right side is just on paper. The Liabilities show us how much we owe other people and the Equity (including the Retained Earnings) simply shows us what portion of the assets are ours free and clear.

Was it a smart strategy to take out that much cash to buy the wagon? No.

Can a business that's profitable get itself in trouble? Absolutely.

Because what runs the business on a daily basis? Do profits? No, cash runs the business on a daily basis!

If you remember nothing else from this book, always remember this!

ON A DAILY BASIS, CASH RUNS THE BUSINESS, NOT PROFITS.

Are profits and cash the same thing? *No.*

What's the thing, the driving force, the blood of the business? *Cash.*

Again, what runs the business? *Cash.*

In truth, the profit just tells you how much you earned. It lets you know that your sales have exceeded your costs. And, when you combine the profits with your original investment it just tells you what portion of your total assets belongs to you.

Can you run a business for a while without profits? *Yes.*

How long can you run a business without cash? *Not one day!*

So, if you were to look at a financial statement and it was typed out with dollar amounts and you saw $52 in retained earnings, you might conclude, "Gee, I must have $52 in a bank account somewhere." Do we have any money in the bank? *No.* That is a really, really important distinction. Our stand has been successful and profitable. We have received a lot of Cash when we made those profits. But we have spent that Cash on Inventory, a building, an insurance policy, a wagon, etc. The Receivables tell us that some of those profits have not yet been turned into Cash because our customers still owe us. Making a profit is very important, but having profits do not mean you have Cash.

And, as fate would have it, it doesn't rain. Everybody crowds around our mobile unit for some lemonade and guess what?

Sales are good! You sell all the pre-made lemonade for $50 cash. Your other Inventory remains the same. You breathe a sigh of relief.

Let's review what just happened.

What goes out? *Inventory for $30.00.*

What comes in? *Cash.*

How much? *$50.00.*

What are our earnings on that? *$20.00.*

And on the Cash Statement, that's what? *Collections.*

Please complete your next Balance Sheet.

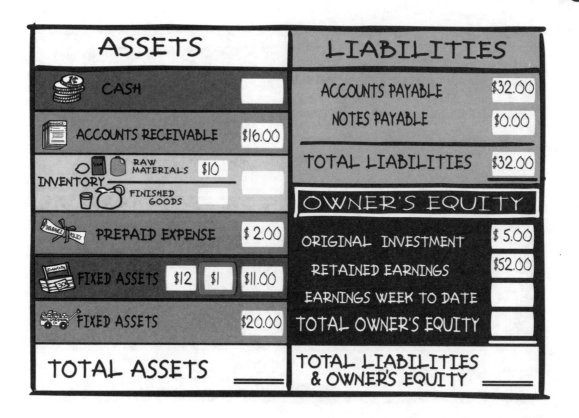

Given that good weather, luck, and a little business savvy saved the day, you decide to pay yourself $4 salary in cash. Finally! It's your fifth week in business and, after what you've been through, you think you deserve it.

What comes out? *$4.00 Cash. Salary to the owner is an expense.*

Which will reduce earnings by how much? *$4.00.*

Complete another Balance Sheet, recording this transaction.

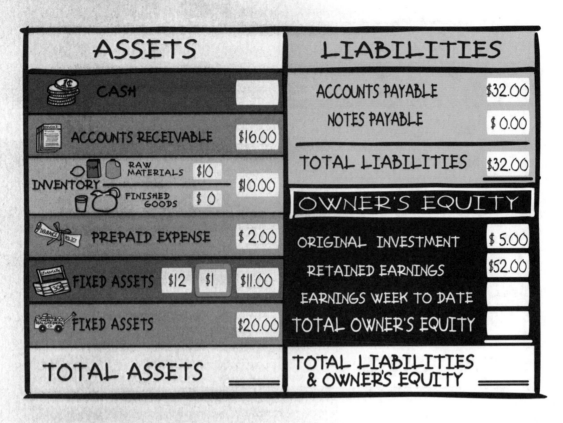

ASSETS			LIABILITIES	
CASH			ACCOUNTS PAYABLE	$32.00
			NOTES PAYABLE	$ 0.00
ACCOUNTS RECEIVABLE		$16.00	TOTAL LIABILITIES	$32.00
INVENTORY RAW MATERIALS $10 FINISHED GOODS $ 0		$10.00	OWNER'S EQUITY	
PREPAID EXPENSE		$ 2.00	ORIGINAL INVESTMENT	$ 5.00
FIXED ASSETS	$12 $1	$11.00	RETAINED EARNINGS	$52.00
FIXED ASSETS		$20.00	EARNINGS WEEK TO DATE	
			TOTAL OWNER'S EQUITY	
TOTAL ASSETS		_____	TOTAL LIABILITIES & OWNER'S EQUITY	_____

Now that you're back on your feet, you can look down the road a little bit. As part of your financial planning, you realize that you have to depreciate the mobile unit—after all, you own it.

What method did we use when we depreciated the building? Straight line depreciation.

This is the only method you can use with a building. With equipment, though, you have a choice. You can use straight line or accelerated depreciation.

For those of you who have done any depreciation of assets over the past few years, you probably recognize that the government often changes the formulas that you use to do depreciation. One formula is called 2x (2 "times"—or multiplied by 2) the straight line base (also called double declining balance). There's another one called one and one-half times the declining balance.

There was a method called ACRS (Accelerated Cost Recovery System). Then there was MACRS (Modified Accelerated Cost Recovery System). The government frequently changes the period of time you can depreciate an asset and the rate at which you can depreciate it. We've elected to use 2x the straight line base as the method we're going to use for accelerated depreciation.

What did we say the life of our wagon will be? Ten years.

What was the cost of the wagon? $20.00.

If we're going to depreciate using straight line, what happens? It is how much per year? $2.00. Straight line equals $2 per year.

We're not using straight line, we're using 2x straight line. What would our depreciation amount be in the first year? $4.00.

If we took $4 off our mobile unit, how do we show that on a Balance Sheet? Reduce the value of the Fixed Asset.

Show this transaction.

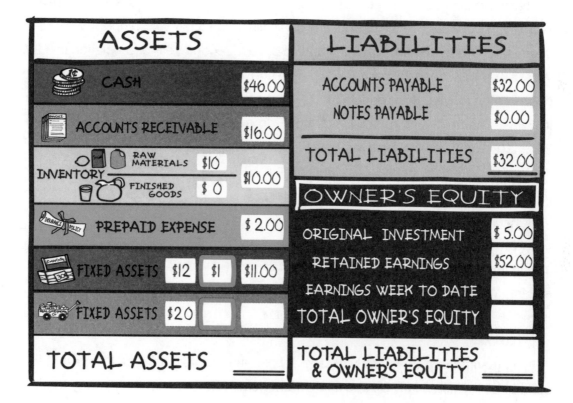

Okay, so our mobile unit is now valued at what? $16.00.

We know now that depreciation is what? An expense.

What do expenses do to earnings? Reduce them. In the case of depreciating the wagon, what will it do to our earnings? Reduce them by $4.00.

Taking them down to what? $12.00.

Will it show up on the cash statement? No. Remember, depreciation is a non-cash expense.

How about the income statement? Yes, as an expense.

So, the first year, instead of taking $2 we're going to take $4.

The key word in the depreciation formula is the word "base."

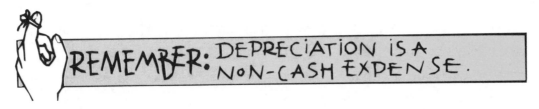

REMEMBER: DEPRECIATION IS A NON-CASH EXPENSE.

What was the cost of the wagon—or its original base? $20.00.

Now, we subtract $4 in year one, what's the new base? $16.00. It's still a ten-year property. What would be the straight line depreciation on a ten-year property with a $16 base? $1.60. That amount, times 2 = 3.20. So, your second year depreciation is 3.20. What's the new base for year 3? $12.80 (subtract 3.20 from 16). The straight line depreciation for year three equals? $1.28. That amount, times 2 is $2.56. You see how it works. The next year is $2.04, etc. If we do a graph, it looks like this…$4, 3.20, 2.56, 2.04…you see it's a curved line.

You're taking a greater amount of the depreciation in the earlier years and taking less depreciation in the later years. Is that good? Yes. Another way to say that is you are saving current tax dollars versus future tax dollars. Why? Because saving current dollars is better than saving future dollars because of inflation.

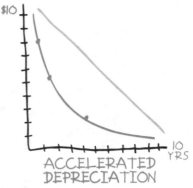

ACCELERATED DEPRECIATION

The government often lets you take accelerated depreciation for things that will need to be replaced early on due to wear and tear. It's the government's way to support businesses in buying and selling assets which stimulates the economy. Those are only some of the reasons for accelerated depreciation.

Now we're going to introduce one final concept that affects all companies—TAXES.

For now, let's just focus on this week's profit. You now owe taxes to the government. Our profits this week are $12. The tax rate is 25 percent. With $12 in earnings taxed at 25 percent, what are the taxes? $3.00.

Which reduces earnings to what? $9.00.

Remember that we said that we owe the taxes, not that we paid them.

Now, create a Balance Sheet, Income Statement, and Cash Statement for this week and include the tax liability. We have printed the Balance Sheet to more closely resemble an actual company balance sheet. See if you can complete it.

ASSETS		LIABILITIES	
Cash	$ _____	Accounts Payable	$ _____
Accounts Receivable	$ _____	Notes Payable	$ _____
		Tax Liability	$ _____
Inventory	$ _____	TOTAL LIABILITIES	$ _____
Prepaid Expenses	$ _____		
Total Current Assets	$ _____	OWNER'S EQUITY	
		Original Investment	$ _____
Gross Fixed Assets	$ _____	Retained Earnings	$ _____
Accumulated Depreciation	$ _____	Earnings Week to Date	$ _____
Net Fixed Assets	$ _____	TOTAL EQUITY	$ _____
		Total Liabilities and	
Total Assets	$ _____	Owner's Equity	$ _____

The Cash, Accounts Receivable, Inventory, and Prepaid Expenses are what are called "Current Assets." Current Assets are those assets that will likely be converted to cash within one year. The total Current Assets are $74.

When you don't have the use of color to show Fixed Assets and depreciation, there are often three entries for Fixed Assets. "Gross Fixed Assets" is the total purchase price of all the fixed assets. "Accumulated Depreciation" represents the total depreciation taken to date on the assets. And the "Net Fixed Assets," of course, is the difference—or what's called the Net Book Value of the assets. One advantage of having all three numbers is the ease by which to compare the accumulated depreciation amount to the Gross Fixed Assets amount. This comparison lets us know that our company's fixed assets are relatively new.

The Net Fixed Assets amount was for how much $27.00.

And the total assets are? $101.00.

The total liabilities, including $3 in Tax Liability is how much? $35.00.

Total equity equals…? $66.00.

Are we in balance? Yes.

Before we do the week's Income Statement and Cash Statement, let's review the transactions one more time.

TRANSACTIONS:

You purchase a mobile lemonade stand for $20 cash. Estimated life of the mobile unit is 10 years.

You purchase some more pre-made lemonade, and the price has increased to $30 cash.

(But, remember, we only had $21 cash and put $9 on account.)

You have sales of 100 glasses of lemonade @ 50¢ /glass, for $50 cash.

You decide to pay yourself a salary for $4 cash.

You depreciate the mobile unit using accelerated depreciation (2 x straight line base). Include all of the first year's depreciation.

You pay 25% of net profit before taxes.

```
INCOME STATEMENT        Begin: Monday A.M.    End: Sunday P.M.
SALES                                              $  _____
      Beginning Inventory             $  _____
      + Purchases                        _____
      + Labor                            _____
      Total Available for Sale       $  _____
      - Ending Inventory                _____
= COST OF GOODS SOLD                               _____
GROSS PROFIT =                                     _____
EXPENSES
      •  _____    _____
      •  _____    _____
      •  _____

= TOTAL EXPENSES                                   _____
NET PROFIT BEFORE TAXES                            _____
INCOME TAXES                                       _____
NET PROFIT AFTER TAXES                          $  _____
```

Okay. Let's review the Income Statement.

Sales? $50.00.

Beginning Inventory? $10.00.

Purchases? $30.00.

Total available for sale? $40.00.

Ending Inventory? $10. Wow! We still got some old and by now highly suspect lemons on the Balance Sheet! We're going to have to figure out what to do with these rotten lemons soon.

Cost of Goods Sold? $30.00.

What's the Gross Profit for the week? $20.00.

Expenses? Salary, $4.00; Depreciation, $4.00.

Total Expenses? $8.00.

So, our Net Profit before taxes? $12.00.

What did Uncle Sam take? $3.00.

Leaving us with a Net Profit After Taxes (NPAT) of...? $9.00.

Now, fill out the week's Cash Statement.

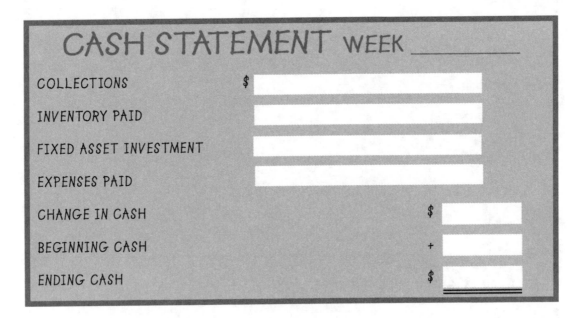

CASH STATEMENT WEEK _____

COLLECTIONS	$
INVENTORY PAID	
FIXED ASSET INVESTMENT	
EXPENSES PAID	
CHANGE IN CASH	$
BEGINNING CASH	+
ENDING CASH	$

What was the change in cash? *Plus five.*

The Beginning Cash was $41, so you should have $46 in Ending Cash. Check to see if you do.

Well, that completes another full week! You're doing great!

You're really enjoying the lemonade business and learning about accounting. Which isn't to say that now you're not ready for a little break. You are, especially when you learn that the family is jumping in the car and heading to one of your favorite destinations. Which is (write the answer below).

_____

Just remember to send us a postcard, okay?

CHAPTER 9

W ell, you and your family had the best time on your trip! You got to order fancy desserts and eat at the sort of restaurants that your parents never take you to when you're home. You got to watch lots of cable television in hotel rooms. You saw all sorts of wild stuff and spent whatever money your parents gave you. You even spent your own hard-earned money, on something that you promised yourself you'd keep forever.

But now, you're home. And—guess what?!—you have to go back to school in a couple of weeks. Summer's almost over.

Time to shake out the mental cobwebs and get ready for reading, writing, and math!

In fact, with school just around the corner, you decide to quit the lemonade business, at least for this summer. Yes, sad to say, it's time to close up shop, pay our bills, and complete your final statements.

For starters, let's look at our last Balance Sheet from last week and correct it for taxes for the summer. Because would we owe taxes on all the earnings? Yes. Here's that last Balance Sheet, for review.

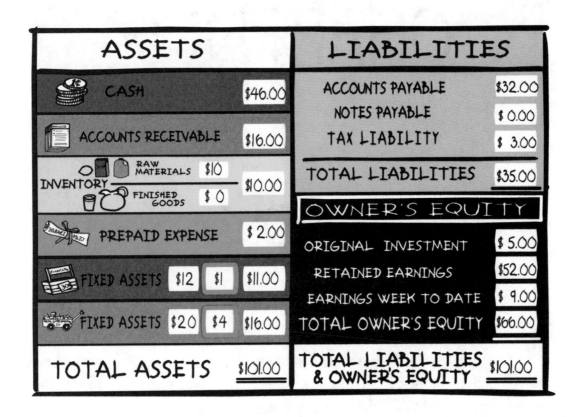

ASSETS				LIABILITIES	
CASH			$46.00	ACCOUNTS PAYABLE	$32.00
				NOTES PAYABLE	$ 0.00
ACCOUNTS RECEIVABLE			$16.00	TAX LIABILITY	$ 3.00
INVENTORY	RAW MATERIALS	$10	$10.00	TOTAL LIABILITIES	$35.00
	FINISHED GOODS	$ 0		**OWNER'S EQUITY**	
PREPAID EXPENSE			$ 2.00	ORIGINAL INVESTMENT	$ 5.00
FIXED ASSETS	$12	$1	$11.00	RETAINED EARNINGS	$52.00
				EARNINGS WEEK TO DATE	$ 9.00
FIXED ASSETS	$20	$4	$16.00	TOTAL OWNER'S EQUITY	$66.00
TOTAL ASSETS			**$101.00**	**TOTAL LIABILITIES & OWNER'S EQUITY**	**$101.00**

Our pre-tax profit last week was $12 (add the $3 tax back into the $9 Earnings Week to Date) and the retained earnings were $52. Adding pre-tax profit and Retained Earnings, our total pretax earnings for the summer are $64. Figure 25 percent as our tax rate. So, our total tax liability is? $16.00.

Now do the new Balance Sheet.

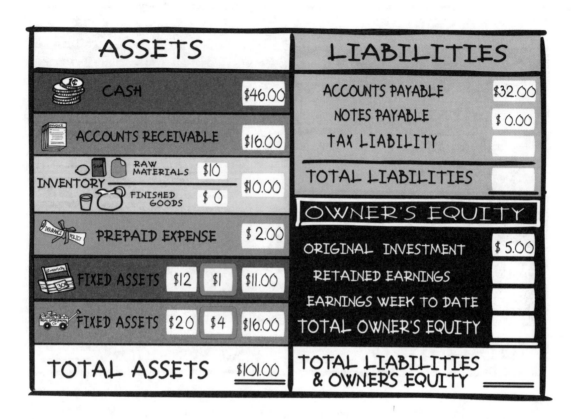

Are we going to leave those old and now very ugly lemons in the family refrigerator? *No way! Mom and Dad want those lemons gone—and soon!*

We have another inventory system we have to look at. It's called FISH. Which stands for, First In, Still Here. And in what condition? *Rotten, very rotten.*

What do we need to do about those lemons? *Throw them out.*

Right. But what do we need to do about those lemons, as far as accounting is concerned? *Write them off.*

Let's get rid of those lemons. What goes off the left side of the Balance Sheet? *Inventory.* And what will that reduce on the right side? *Earnings.*

Go ahead.

ASSETS					LIABILITIES	
CASH				$46.00	ACCOUNTS PAYABLE	$32.00
					NOTES PAYABLE	$ 0.00
ACCOUNTS RECEIVABLE				$16.00	TAX LIABILITY	
INVENTORY	RAW MATERIALS				TOTAL LIABILITIES	
	FINISHED GOODS	$ 0			OWNER'S EQUITY	
PREPAID EXPENSE				$ 2.00	ORIGINAL INVESTMENT	$ 5.00
FIXED ASSETS	$12	$1	$11.00		RETAINED EARNINGS	
					EARNINGS WEEK TO DATE	
FIXED ASSETS	$20	$4	$16.00		TOTAL OWNER'S EQUITY	
TOTAL ASSETS				___	TOTAL LIABILITIES & OWNER'S EQUITY	___

Problem? If so, look at the tax liabilities as a likely source. Why? Would the $10 write off of inventory affect taxes? Yes. See if you can recalculate earnings and taxes (round off to the next dollar).

BEFORE WRITE-OFF	
EARNINGS	TAXES @ 25%
$_____	$_____
AFTER WRITE-OFF	
EARNINGS	TAXES @ 25%
$_____	$_____

Now, if necessary, make any corrections to the last Balance Sheet.

Are we in balance now? Yes.

How are we going to write the inventory off on the Income Statement? You may say, "Expense them"—however, what's our ending inventory now? Zero.

Instead of expensing it, we are going to write it off...where? Ending Inventory.

Reduce it to zero. We write it off in inventory because it's the cost of our product or inventory.

As a result, this week's Income Statement would have higher Cost of Goods Sold and lower Gross Profit.

Earlier, when we were doing our statements during these weeks, have we been a little creative about the value of our inventory? Yes.

Have our assets possibly been overstated? Yes.

Did the lemons go bad? Yes.

Do you know exactly when they went bad? No, not exactly. We really don't know if it was the second, third, or fourth week. True. So, when should we have written them off? Hard to say exactly.

What should have happened the moment the lemons went bad? We should have thrown them away and written off the loss then.

All that time when we went to our banker without statements, what were we doing? We were overstating or inflating the true value of our assets.

By how much? $10.00.

What else were we overstating? Our Earnings.

Because we should have put what there for ending inventory? Zero, a long time ago.

What happens if your inventory is widgets? Or nuts and bolts, or anything that is not perishable? And you want to know if it's good or bad? If you went to the warehouse, what would you look for? Dust. And what else could you have on there? Cobwebs, maybe.

If you're planning to buy a company or loan money to a company and you're going to go and look at inventory, what are you going to look for? Cobwebs and dust. And then, what are you going to know about that inventory? It's old.

And what else? It's not selling very well!

Now, let's just say it's your business, and you want to sell your business. And you've got this inventory, what are you going to do? For starters, clean it.

Right, get the vacuum cleaner out. Move the inventory around the shelves to make sure you get all the dust off. You want it to look pristine.

What have we here? Have we another area where people are sometimes creative?

When you go to your Balance Sheet, how do you find out how much cash is in the business? You count it.

How do you find out about the Accounts Receivables? *You check the books or call the customers up to see if they agree how much they owe.*

Prepaid Insurance Policy? *Read the policy to see what the dates are.*

The stand? *Go out and look at it.*

Easy to determine if they're still good or not, right? *Right.*

Inventory, on the other hand, is the toughest part to determine when you're buying or selling a business. This is where you need the most expertise and help, because lots of people get creative in how they present their inventory. If you're ever in the position of buying or selling a business that involves inventory get an expert in to help determine its true value.

Mom's always harping about keeping our room clean. Especially if you're ever trying to sell the house. The same is true in business. So, let's clean up our Balance Sheet.

How much do we owe our suppliers? *$32.00.* Let's pay them.

And let's pay off our taxes of $14.00.

Let's collect the $16.00 dollars still due in receivables.

Let's also cancel the insurance policy and receive a $2 refund.

Okay. On the next Balance Sheet, demonstrate where we stand at the end of the summer.

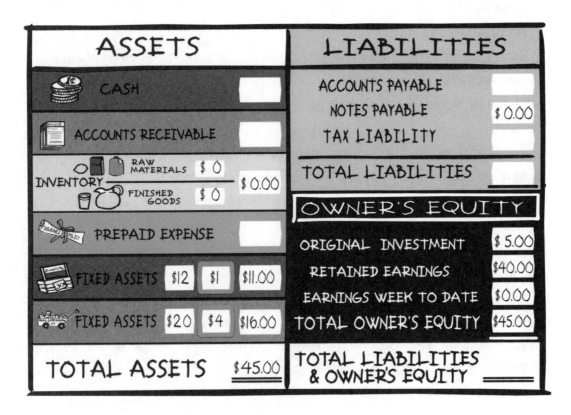

We still have our $5 original investment and $40 in earnings—for $45 in total equity. But we only have how much cash? $18.00.

Again, you can see the lesson we learned earlier. You have $45 in Equity, but only $18 in Cash. And why is that? Because $27 in Equity is tied up in the building and the wagon.

Still, are we in good shape for next year? Or, should we liquidate the building and wagon? It's an option.

It is an option. If you decide to stay in the lemonade business you are all set for next summer with your stand and wagon. Of course, the downside is you've only got $18 Cash—not that great.

If you decide to liquidate the building and wagon you need to find a buyer, which could be difficult. That's why these two are last in the order of Assets. In general, Assets are organized on the Balance Sheet in descending order of Liquidity. (Liquidity means how quickly something can be converted to cash.)

If you sell the Fixed Assets for more than book value, you have to recognize the "gain" as profit. If they are sold for less than book value, you recognize the "loss."

Okay, do a final, Income Statement for the whole summer. To do this you need to get information from the previous five week's income statements.

YEAR-TO-DATE INCOME STATEMENT	Begin:	End:
SALES		$
Beginning Inventory	$	
+ Purchases		
+ Labor		
Total Available for Sale	$	
- Ending Inventory		
= COST OF GOODS SOLD		
GROSS PROFIT =		
EXPENSES		
• Glass Rental		
• Advertising		
• Rent		
• Bad Debt		
• Interest		
• Insurance		
• Paint		
• Roof Repair		
• Depreciation		
• Salary		
= TOTAL EXPENSES		
NET PROFIT BEFORE TAXES		
INCOME TAXES		
NET PROFIT AFTER TAXES		$

So, is that the end of it? Is that the end of our lemonade business? Our plans to build a great commercial empire? No, not quite.

Before we gear up for back to school, we need to do some analysis regarding what we accomplished this summer.

CHAPTER 10

Over the summer, we learned a lot of accounting skills; no question. Now, let's use the experience of running our own business and think about things on a slightly higher level. It's one thing to be able to do something. It's another thing to be able to understand the big lessons involved in doing something.

So far in this book, we've learned about the three financial statements—the Balance Sheet, the Income Statement, and the Cash Statement. We've learned how each is structured, its purpose and relationships to the other two. We've also learned how to separate Cost of Goods or Cost of Services from Expenses. We learned the Accrual versus Cash Method of accounting, service company accounting, capitalizing versus expensing, depreciation, and Cash versus Earnings. What bottom line have we focused on all book long? Net Profit.

Now that you know all you've learned so far, you may be wondering, how did my lemonade stand really do and how do I find out how I did?

Let's begin by asking you to review how the summer went and how you feel about your stand and its performance overall. Take a moment to reflect on this and write down your thoughts.

_____

_____

_____

Is there anything you would have done differently?

_____

_____

_____

_____

Did you work hard? Did the business grow? Did you make money? What are the things you did and decisions you made at the lemonade stand that affected profit positively or negatively?

_____

_____

_____

_____

_____

Many things happened that influenced profits. Compare this list to what you wrote. We hired our best friend to make advertising signs rather than do them ourselves. We decided to make our own lemonade. Later we hired our sister to make some of the lemonade—did we negotiate the right price for labor? We went on a vacation and had to sell some inventory at cost—would you have wanted to give up the vacation? We sold to some customers with questionable credit and got stiffed. We borrowed money and had to pay interest. We chose the LIFO method which gave the illusion of lower profits. We bought property that required maintenance and depreciation. We bought pre-made lemonade and paid more for it than it would have cost to make the lemonade ourselves. We decided to open a new business opportunity at the ball game. We had to pay more to buy lemonade at the grocer near the ballpark. We successfully negotiated credit to get the lemonade when our cash was low. We forgot to use some the lemons we bought and they spoiled.

All of these decisions had a direct impact on our company's profit.

Could you have done better? Now that you look at all the above, do you feel any disappointment in your summer's performance?

Here's the real question. Whether you own your company or work as an employee for a company, do you make decisions that affect your company's profits? Truly, does any person in an organization not have an affect on company profitability?

Does whether or not your company make a profit affect you personally? How?

_____

_____

_____

_____

How often do you think about how your actions and decisions affect profits? Daily? Weekly? Monthly? Yearly? Never?

_____

_____

_____

_____

What does it mean for a company to be making a profit? What are the benefits of profit?

_____

_____

_____

_____

What are decisions that have been made in your department or company that have affected profits?

_____

_____

_____

_____

We've talked about profits throughout this book and you probably recognize by now that of the three financial statements, the Income Statement provides the clearest picture of profit. But in the last chapter, we said on a daily basis, cash runs the business, not profits. So which is more important—cash or profits? Cash runs the business and profit is the bottom line. Cash is not even mentioned on the Income Statement. Does all of this seem a little confusing? If it is, then great. Please let yourself live in this apparent paradox and feel its discomfort for awhile. Living in this paradox and resolving its seeming conflicts is a great part of the art and science of business leadership and success.

Part of the problem is that many of us do not understand what profit really is. We know from the last chapter what cash is. It is so tangible and measurable. Profit is also measurable, however it is not real—it's just a theory.

I bet that shakes up your brains a little. So how do I mean it's not real?

Let's take some examples from our lemonade stand. In Week Two we sold some lemonade and made a profit. It certainly was measurable and we recorded it in our financial statements. But then a customer who owed us $4 moved away from town (or went bankrupt) and $4 of our profits disappeared just like that. So even though you have profits today, tomorrow they can vanish.

At the end of the summer we had $10 worth of old lemons that we let spoil. We had to throw them out and another $10 of our profits disappeared.

Imagine that the wagon didn't work out, and we discontinued the idea of selling at the little league games. Businesses make mistakes all the time or stop a venture they've started. We would have had to write off the $20 for the wagon as another loss to profits unless we could have found a buyer for the wagon.

Profits are easily and clearly measurable so they can readily be used by businesses as an objective measure of efficiency, productivity, and innovation. Their vulnerability to being lost is certainly one reason business leaders want so much to enroll their employees in maximizing and preserving company profitability.

But many employees do not truly understand profits and certainly do not know measures they can use to guide decisions and behavior.

To discover these, let's go back to the Income Statement whose bottom line is Net Profit. What are the three other major items on the Income Statement that affect profits?

_____

_____

_____

Profits are not real because they only exist on paper. Go to any business and ask them to show you some profits. They can't do it. They can show you assets – cash, inventory, fixed assets, etc. These assets increase or decrease when companies make profits or losses.

Sales, Cost of Goods/Services, and Expenses. Profit by definition is the amount by which your sales exceed your costs of providing the goods or services and to run the business. Your company's sales measure how much your customers are willing to vote (with their cash) for your product or service. The two cost categories measure how motivated and effective the company's employees are in making decisions and managing the operation.

If you look at the three measures, how do you increase profits?

_____

_____

_____

The obvious answer is to increase sales and decrease Cost of Goods/Services and Expenses. We all know that none of these is an absolute. We would not want to increase sales on a product that gives a very low profit margin or if we were unable to meet the increased production schedule. We might want to increase Costs of Goods and Expenses if we're starting up a new line of production.

So what do you measure and use to guide decisions if you work on a production line or in an administrative department?

It certainly begins with Sales, COGS, and Expenses, but the raw numbers for these presents a problem. Look at the numbers for our summer at the lemonade stand and see if you can discover the problem in just using the raw numbers.

Since we artificially eliminated Expenses in week three, the chart below is going to compare weeks 1, 2, 4, and 5.

Week	I	II	IV	V
TREND ANALYSIS				
Sales	25	32	50	50
COGS	10	15	20	30
Expenses	5	7	6	8
Net Profit	10	10	24	12

The problem is that from period to period the numbers are not stable—they fluctuate. Fluctuations in these numbers occur for many reasons—seasonally (we sell more lemonade in summer than winter), normal business cycle, marketing campaigns, etc.

What can we do to give us better numbers to work with that take out the fluctuations?

_____

_____

_____

_____

We hope that your answer was to use comparisons or ratios. Regardless of whether the numbers are increasing or decreasing, we can get consistency by comparing Cost of Goods to Sales, Expenses to Sales, and Net Profit to Sales. Let's look at these numbers for week 5. Sales were $50, Cost of Goods $30, Expenses $8, and Net Profit $12 (pre-tax).

The three ratios are:

$$\frac{\text{Cost of Goods}}{\text{Sales}} = \frac{30}{50} = .60 \text{ or } 60\%$$

$$\frac{\text{Expenses}}{\text{Sales}} = \frac{8}{50} = .16 \text{ or } 16\%$$

$$\frac{\text{Net Profit}}{\text{Sales}} \quad = \quad \frac{12}{50} \quad = \quad .24 \text{ or } 24\%$$

What do these mean? Out of every dollar in Sales, it costs us 60 cents for the goods for the sale, 16 cents to run the business, and we make 24 cents in Net Profit.

But are these numbers good or bad? We need still more comparison. And what would we compare to?

_____

_____

First, our competitors, and since different industries and different types of businesses have different ratios, it's important that we compare ourselves to our true competitors.

How do we find out our competitors' numbers, so we can do a competitive analysis? Should we simply call them up and ask for their ratios? Not likely! Well, this may take a little library or Internet research—because several companies keep a record of Industry Ratios and Norms. Dunn & Bradstreet and Robert Morris & Associates are two that keep key rations and industry norms.

Getting this information compares us to competitors, but who else did we say we want to compare to? Ourselves.

How are we to compare ourselves to ourselves? Let's use a sports team, the Chicago Bulls, as an analogy. If they won last night, what does that tell us? Certainly, we may be happy they won (if we're fans), but does that make them a good team all of the time? What if they lost last night? Does that make them a bad team?

The point is, looking at a single game doesn't tell us much. What will tell us more? A season would tell us quite a bit more. But the best indicator of the whole organization would be several seasons—i.e., a trend.

In business we would call this analysis a "trend analysis."

In this book, we've taken the liberty of using weeks as our accounting period. In a real life, a trend analysis would use years. So, we're going to use four weeks and pretend they are years, just to show you how it works. Since we had no expenses in week three, we will leave that week out and look at weeks 1, 2, 4, and 5.

The trend analysis table will show us our Sales, Cost of Goods, Expenses, and Net Profit. It will also show our three ratios: COGS/Sales, Expenses/Sales, and Net Profit/Sales.

TREND ANALYSIS

Week	I	II	IV	V
Sales	25	32	50	50
COGS	10	15	20	30
Expenses	5	7	6	8
Net Profit	10	10	24	12

RATIOS

	I	II	IV	V
COGS/Sales	$\frac{10}{25} = .4$	$\frac{15}{32} = .47$	$\frac{20}{50} = .4$	$\frac{30}{50} = .6$
Exp./Sales	$\frac{5}{25} = .2$	$\frac{7}{32} = .22$	$\frac{6}{50} = .12$	$\frac{8}{50} = .16$
NP/Sales	$\frac{10}{25} = .4$	$\frac{10}{32} = .31$	$\frac{24}{32} = .48$	$\frac{12}{50} = .24$

Now, using our key ratios, review the trend analysis table and answer the following questions:

1. Did we make a profit? _____

2. How is the Net Profit/Sales trending, up or down? _____

3. If the Net Profit/Sales ratio is going down, is the problem reflected in the COGS/Sales ratio, the Expenses/Sales ratio, or both? _____

4. What has been happening in the business that is causing the problem?

_____

_____

5. As a business leader, how would you resolve the problem?

_____

_____

_____

_____

Now, let's review the questions. We did make a profit each week this summer. However, with a Net Profit/Sales ratio that went from 0.4 to 0.24, this ratio was going down, which is a problem. Looking at the two cost ratios, we see that although there was some fluctuation in the Expenses/Sales ratio, it was pretty steady over the four periods. The problem is in COGS/Sales which went from 0.4 to 0.6, a very dramatic increase.

What has happened in the business to cause the problem? The easy answer is that the cost of lemonade was a lot higher at the grocer near the game than at your regular grocer's. From the larger perspective, you made a rash and poorly planned decision to start a new venture. There was no plan to continue the stand which was making money, while starting the new venture at the game. Purchasing the equipment almost put you out of business and certainly had an indirect effect on profit. There was very poor planning about the purchase of new inventory and the cash shortage limited your options and negotiating power at the new grocery store. Finally, you failed to recognize that people pay a lot more for drinks at a game and did not raise your prices accordingly, which could have lessened the pain of your increased costs. It should now be fairly clear what you would do differently.

How do you like being a consultant? You're pretty darn smart, aren't you? You should feel pretty happy to have the tools to analyze your and other company's profit performance and the key questions that can lead to discovering how to improve it. You can now go back to the list of things that affected profit and prioritize the things you would change or do differently.

Do you think there are other important bottom lines besides Net Profit? Yes.

You're right. We think there are three crucial bottom lines needed to measure the health of a business. In this book, we examined one of them, Net Profit. For those who are interested in working with all three, Educational Discoveries has a workshop called the Financial Game for Decision Making. After participating in the Financial Game for Decision Making, you will know not only the three critical bottom lines, but the six crucial drivers of these bottom lines. You will then know how to focus the efforts of your work force to maximize the financial performance of your company. For more information on this, call us at 1-800-808-4136.

Hey! We still need to complete *The Accounting Game.* To do so, please take the Post-Test. You'll recognize it as the same as the Pre-Test you took at the start of this book. But we guarantee that your score will be a lot higher now! Take a few minutes and complete the test. When you're done, you'll find the answers at the end of this book. Score both the Pre- and Post-Test. Then congratulate yourself on how much you've learned!

Post-Test

1. Which one of the following items is not found on a Balance Sheet?
   - A. Cash
   - B. Gross Profit
   - C. Assets
   - D. Liabilities

2. Which accounting system most accurately reflects profitability?
   - A. Cash Accounting
   - B. Flow of Funds Accounting
   - C. Accrual Accounting

3. An account receivable is:
   - A. an Asset
   - B. Owner's Equity
   - C. a Liability

4. Which of the following is most important to the daily operations of a business?
   - A. Assets
   - B. Retained Earnings
   - C. Cash

5. When people speak about the bottom line, they are referring to:
   - A. Net Profit
   - B. Gross Margin
   - C. Gross Profit

6. A prepaid expense is:

    A. an Asset   B. Owner's Equity

    C. a Liability

7. Is LIFO/FIFO a method of:

    A. Inventory Evaluation   B. Profit Ratio

    C. Financing

8. Which would you find on an Income Statement?

    A. Expense   B. Fixed Asset

    C. Liability

9. Which of the following expenses does not affect your cash position in running a business:

    A. Lease Expense   B. Advertising Expense

    C. Depreciation Expense

10. Which of the following is a basic accounting equation:

    A. Net Worth = Assets + Profits

    B. Gross Profit - Sales = Gross Profit Margin

    C. Assets = Liabilities + Owner's Equity

Now, there's one last thing. What do you get at the end of school? A *diploma.*
On the last page of the book is a diploma, signifying your successful completion of *The Accounting Game.*

Fill it out. Then tape it to your desk at work. Hang it on your refrigerator. Frame it and nail it above your bed. Or, best of all, proudly post it on your own, real-life lemonade stand next summer!

Answer Key

Answers to Chapter One

Page 10

50 lemons at 20¢ each = $10.00

5 pounds of sugar at 40¢ per pound = $2.00

2 gallons of water   free

Total Purchases = $12.00

Page 11

50 lemons @ 20¢ each $10.00

5 lbs. Sugar @ 40¢ lb. $2.00

+ 2 gal. Water   No Charge

60 Glasses = $12.00

COST of Production $12 = Cost Per Unit (Glass) $.20
# of Glasses 60

Page 13

Sales $25.00

Cost of Goods Sold (50 glasses @ 20¢ each) - $10.00

Gross Profit (Earnings so far) $15.00

Page 15

Glass Rental $2.00
Advertising $1.00
Rent $2.00
Total Expenses = $5.00

Answers to Chapter Two

Page 24

Sales $25.00
- COGS $10.00
Gross Profit $15.00
- Expenses $5.00
Net Profit $10.00

Answers to Chapter Three

Page 38

ASSETS		LIABILITIES	
CASH	$63.00	NOTES PAYABLE	$50.00
		TOTAL LIABILITIES	$50.00
INVENTORY	$2.00	**OWNER'S EQUITY**	
		ORIGINAL INVESTMENT	$5.00
		RETAINED EARNINGS	$10.00
		EARNINGS WEEK TO DATE	$0.00
		TOTAL OWNER'S EQUITY	$15.00
TOTAL ASSETS	$65.00	TOTAL LIABILITIES & OWNER'S EQUITY	$65.00

Page 39

ASSETS		LIABILITIES	
CASH	$65.00	ACCOUNTS PAYABLE	$50.00
		TOTAL LIABILITIES	$50.00
INVENTORY	$0.00	**OWNER'S EQUITY**	
		ORIGINAL INVESTMENT	$5.00
		RETAINED EARNINGS	$10.00
		EARNINGS WEEK TO DATE	$0.00
		TOTAL OWNER'S EQUITY	$15.00
TOTAL ASSETS	$65.00	TOTAL LIABILITIES & OWNER'S EQUITY	$65.00

Page 42

ASSETS		LIABILITIES	
CASH	$65.00	ACCOUNTS PAYABLE	$4.00
		NOTES PAYABLE	$50.00
INVENTORY	$4.00	TOTAL LIABILITIES	$54.00
		OWNER'S EQUITY	
		ORIGINAL INVESTMENT	$5.00
		RETAINED EARNINGS	$10.00
		EARNINGS WEEK TO DATE	$0.00
		TOTAL OWNER'S EQUITY	$15.00
TOTAL ASSETS	$69.00	TOTAL LIABILITIES & OWNER'S EQUITY	$69.00

Page 43

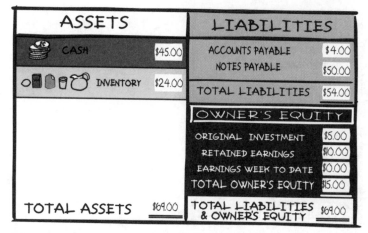

ASSETS		LIABILITIES	
CASH	$45.00	ACCOUNTS PAYABLE	$4.00
		NOTES PAYABLE	$50.00
INVENTORY	$24.00	TOTAL LIABILITIES	$54.00
		OWNER'S EQUITY	
		ORIGINAL INVESTMENT	$5.00
		RETAINED EARNINGS	$10.00
		EARNINGS WEEK TO DATE	$0.00
		TOTAL OWNER'S EQUITY	$15.00
TOTAL ASSETS	$69.00	TOTAL LIABILITIES & OWNER'S EQUITY	$69.00

Answers to Chapter Four

Page 46

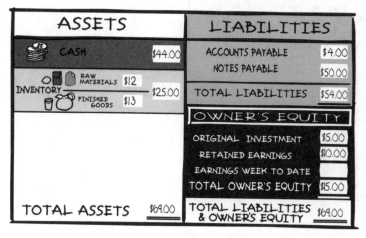

ASSETS		LIABILITIES	
CASH	$44.00	ACCOUNTS PAYABLE	$4.00
		NOTES PAYABLE	$50.00
INVENTORY — RAW MATERIALS $12 / FINISHED GOODS $13	$25.00	TOTAL LIABILITIES	$54.00
		OWNER'S EQUITY	
		ORIGINAL INVESTMENT	$5.00
		RETAINED EARNINGS	$10.00
		EARNINGS WEEK TO DATE	
		TOTAL OWNER'S EQUITY	$15.00
TOTAL ASSETS	$69.00	TOTAL LIABILITIES & OWNER'S EQUITY	$69.00

Page 50

ASSETS		LIABILITIES	
CASH	$64.00	ACCOUNTS PAYABLE	$4.00
		NOTES PAYABLE	$50.00
ACCOUNTS RECEIVABLE	$10.00	TOTAL LIABILITIES	$54.00
INVENTORY — RAW MATERIALS $12 / FINISHED GOODS $0	$12.00	OWNER'S EQUITY	
		ORIGINAL INVESTMENT	$5.00
		RETAINED EARNINGS	$10.00
		EARNINGS WEEK TO DATE	$17.00
		TOTAL OWNER'S EQUITY	$32.00
TOTAL ASSETS	$86.00	TOTAL LIABILITIES & OWNER'S EQUITY	$86.00

Page 52

ASSETS		LIABILITIES	
CASH	$64.00	ACCOUNTS PAYABLE	$4.00
		NOTES PAYABLE	$50.00
ACCOUNTS RECEIVABLE	$6.00	TOTAL LIABILITIES	$54.00
INVENTORY — RAW MATERIALS $12 / FINISHED GOODS $0	$12.00	OWNER'S EQUITY	
		ORIGINAL INVESTMENT	$5.00
		RETAINED EARNINGS	$10.00
		EARNINGS WEEK TO DATE	$13.00
		TOTAL OWNER'S EQUITY	$28.00
TOTAL ASSETS	$82.00	TOTAL LIABILITIES & OWNER'S EQUITY	$82.00

Page 53

ASSETS		LIABILITIES	
CASH	$37.00	ACCOUNTS PAYABLE	$4.00
		NOTES PAYABLE	$25.00
ACCOUNTS RECEIVABLE	$6.00	TOTAL LIABILITIES	$29.00
INVENTORY — RAW MATERIALS $12 / FINISHED GOODS $0	$12.00	OWNER'S EQUITY	
		ORIGINAL INVESTMENT	$5.00
		RETAINED EARNINGS	$10.00
		EARNINGS WEEK TO DATE	$11.00
		TOTAL OWNER'S EQUITY	$26.00
TOTAL ASSETS	$55.00	TOTAL LIABILITIES & OWNER'S EQUITY	$55.00

Page 57

ASSETS			LIABILITIES	
CASH		$34.00	ACCOUNTS PAYABLE	$4.00
			NOTES PAYABLE	$25.00
ACCOUNTS RECEIVABLE		$6.00	TOTAL LIABILITIES	$29.00
INVENTORY	RAW MATERIALS $12	$12.00	**OWNER'S EQUITY**	
	FINISHED GOODS $0		ORIGINAL INVESTMENT	$5.00
			RETAINED EARNINGS	$10.00
PREPAID EXPENSE		$2.00	EARNINGS WEEK TO DATE	
			TOTAL OWNER'S EQUITY	$25.00
TOTAL ASSETS		**$54.00**	**TOTAL LIABILITIES & OWNER'S EQUITY**	**$54.00**

Page 63

ACCRUAL INCOME STATEMENT	Begin: Monday A.M. End: Sunday P.M.		
SALES			$32.00
Beginning Inventory (lemons + sugar or lemonade)		$2.00	
+ Purchases	sugar	$4.00	
	lemons	$20.00	
+ Labor		$1.00	
Total available for sale			$27.00
- Ending Inventory (lemons + sugar or lemonade not sold)			
120 - 60 = 60 glasses x .20 =			$12.00
= COST OF GOODS SOLD			$15.00
GROSS PROFIT =			$17.00
EXPENSES			
• Bad debt		$4.00	
• Interest Expense		$2.00	
• Insurance Express		$1.00	
= TOTAL EXPENSES			$7.00
NET PROFIT (Gross Profit - Expenses)			$10.00

Page 67

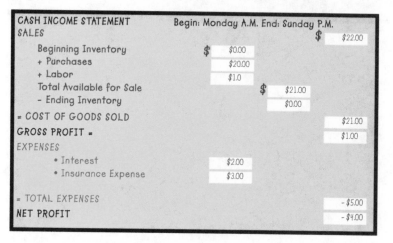

CASH INCOME STATEMENT	Begin: Monday A.M. End: Sunday P.M.		
SALES		$	$22.00
Beginning Inventory	$	$0.00	
+ Purchases		$20.00	
+ Labor		$1.0	
Total Available for Sale	$	$21.00	
- Ending Inventory		$0.00	
= COST OF GOODS SOLD			$21.00
GROSS PROFIT =			$1.00
EXPENSES			
• Interest		$2.00	
• Insurance Expense		$3.00	
= TOTAL EXPENSES			- $5.00
NET PROFIT			- $4.00

ANSWERS TO CHAPTER SIX

Page 80

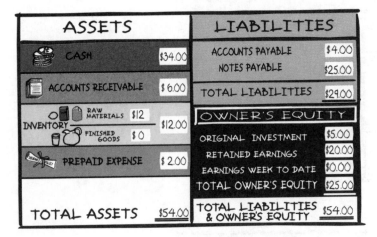

ASSETS		LIABILITIES	
CASH	$34.00	ACCOUNTS PAYABLE	$4.00
		NOTES PAYABLE	$25.00
ACCOUNTS RECEIVABLE	$6.00	TOTAL LIABILITIES	$29.00
INVENTORY — RAW MATERIALS $12	$12.00	**OWNER'S EQUITY**	
— FINISHED GOODS $0		ORIGINAL INVESTMENT	$5.00
		RETAINED EARNINGS	$20.00
PREPAID EXPENSE	$2.00	EARNINGS WEEK TO DATE	$0.00
		TOTAL OWNER'S EQUITY	$25.00
TOTAL ASSETS	$54.00	TOTAL LIABILITIES & OWNER'S EQUITY	$54.00

Page 83

Cost of Production using FIFO: $12.00

Page 86

FIFO INCOME STATEMENT		Begin: Monday A.M. End: Sunday P.M.	
SALES			$30.00
Beginning Inventory	$12.00		
+ Purchases	$20.00		
= Total Available for Sale	$32.00		
- Ending Inventory		$20.00	
		$12.00	
= COST OF GOODS SOLD			
GROSS PROFIT =			$18.00
TOTAL EXPENSES			$0.00
NET PROFIT			$18.00

Page 88

Cost of Production using LIFO: $22.00

Page 90

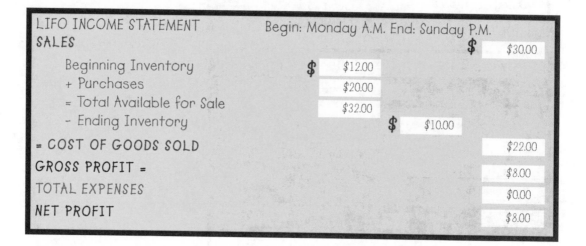

ASSETS		LIABILITIES	
CASH	$59.00	ACCOUNTS PAYABLE	$24.00
		NOTES PAYABLE	$25.00
ACCOUNTS RECEIVABLE	$11.00	TOTAL LIABILITIES	$49.00
INVENTORY — RAW MATERIALS $10 / FINISHED GOODS $0	$10.00	**OWNER'S EQUITY**	
		ORIGINAL INVESTMENT	$5.00
PREPAID EXPENSE	$2.00	RETAINED EARNINGS	$20.00
		EARNINGS WEEK TO DATE	$8.00
		TOTAL OWNER'S EQUITY	$33.00
TOTAL ASSETS	$82.00	**TOTAL LIABILITIES & OWNER'S EQUITY**	$82.00

LIFO INCOME STATEMENT   Begin: Monday A.M. End: Sunday P.M.

SALES		$ $30.00
Beginning Inventory	$ $12.00	
+ Purchases	$20.00	
= Total Available for Sale	$32.00	
- Ending Inventory	$ $10.00	
= COST OF GOODS SOLD		$22.00
GROSS PROFIT =		$8.00
TOTAL EXPENSES		$0.00
NET PROFIT		$8.00

Page 91

	FIFO	LIFO
SALES	$30.00	$30.00
COGS (Cost of Goods Sold)	$12.00	$22.00
PROFIT	$18.00	$8.00
ENDING INVENTORY	$20.00	$10.00

ANSWERS TO CHAPTER SEVEN

Page 99

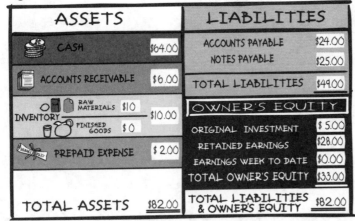

Page 106

Page 109

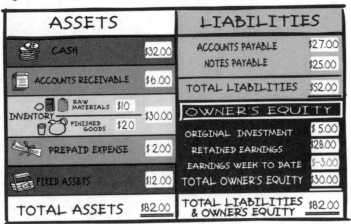

Page 109

CASH STATEMENT WEEK _____

COLLECTIONS	+ $5.00 A/R
INVENTORY PAID	- $20.00 Pre-made
FIXED ASSET	-$10.00 Stand and Land
EXPENSES PAID	- $2.00 Paint
CHANGE IN CASH	
BEGINNING CASH	+ $59.00
ENDING CASH	

Page 113

CASH STATEMENT WEEK _____

COLLECTIONS	+ $5.00 + $40.00
INVENTORY PAID	- $20.00 -$4.00
INVESTMENT	-$10.00
EXPENSES PAID	- $2.00 -$2.00
BORROW/PAY BACK	-$25.00
CHANGE IN CASH	
BEGINNING CASH	$59.00
ENDING CASH	+

Page 115

ASSETS		LIABILITIES	
CASH	$41.00	ACCOUNTS PAYABLE	$23.00
		NOTES PAYABLE	$0.00
ACCOUNTS RECEIVABLE	$16.00	TOTAL LIABILITIES	$23.00
INVENTORY — RAW MATERIALS $10 / FINISHED GOODS $0	$10.00	OWNER'S EQUITY	
PREPAID EXPENSE	$2.00	ORIGINAL INVESTMENT	$5.00
		RETAINED EARNINGS	$28.00
		EARNINGS WEEK TO DATE	$24.00
FIXED ASSETS	$11.00	TOTAL OWNER'S EQUITY	$57.00
TOTAL ASSETS	$80.00	TOTAL LIABILITIES & OWNER'S EQUITY	$80.00

Page 117

CASH STATEMENT WEEK _____

COLLECTIONS	+ $5.00 + $40.00
INVENTORY PAID	- $20.00 - $4.00
INVESTMENT	- $10.00
EXPENSES PAID	- $2.00 - $2.00
BORROW/PAY BACK	- $25.00
CHANGE IN CASH (+45 - 63)	- $18.00
BEGINNING CASH	$59.00
ENDING CASH	+ $41.00

Page 119

INCOME STATEMENT	Begin: Monday A.M. End: Sunday P.M.		
SALES		$	$50.00
Beginning Inventory	$10.00		
+ Purchases	$20.00		
= Total Available for Sale	$30.00		
- Ending Inventory		$10.00	
= COST OF GOODS SOLD			$20.00
GROSS PROFIT =			$30.00
EXPENSES			
Paint	$2.00		
Roof Repair	$1.00		
Interest	$2.00		
Depreciation	$`1.00		$6.00
TOTAL EXPENSES			$24.00
NET PROFIT			

ANSWERS TO CHAPTER EIGHT

Page 122

ASSETS		LIABILITIES	
CASH	$41.00	ACCOUNTS PAYABLE	$23.00
		NOTES PAYABLE	$0.00
ACCOUNTS RECEIVABLE	$16.00		
		TOTAL LIABILITIES	$23.00
INVENTORY — RAW MATERIALS $10 / FINISHED GOODS $0	$10.00	**OWNER'S EQUITY**	
PREPAID EXPENSE	$2.00	ORIGINAL INVESTMENT	$5.00
		RETAINED EARNINGS	$52.00
		EARNINGS WEEK TO DATE	$0.00
FIXED ASSETS $12 $1	$11.00	TOTAL OWNER'S EQUITY	$57.00
TOTAL ASSETS	$80.00	TOTAL LIABILITIES & OWNER'S EQUITY	$80.00

Page 128

ASSETS		LIABILITIES	
CASH	$0.00	ACCOUNTS PAYABLE	$32.00
		NOTES PAYABLE	$0.00
ACCOUNTS RECEIVABLE	$16.00		
INVENTORY — RAW MATERIALS $10 / FINISHED GOODS $30	$40.00	TOTAL LIABILITIES	$32.00
		OWNER'S EQUITY	
PREPAID EXPENSE	$2.00	ORIGINAL INVESTMENT	$5.00
FIXED ASSETS $12 $1	$11.00	RETAINED EARNINGS	$52.00
		EARNINGS WEEK TO DATE	$0.00
FIXED ASSETS	$20.00	TOTAL OWNER'S EQUITY	$57.00
TOTAL ASSETS	$89.00	TOTAL LIABILITIES & OWNER'S EQUITY	$89.00

Page 131

ASSETS		LIABILITIES	
CASH	$50.00	ACCOUNTS PAYABLE	$32.00
		NOTES PAYABLE	$0.00
ACCOUNTS RECEIVABLE	$16.00		
INVENTORY — RAW MATERIALS $10 / FINISHED GOODS $0	$10.00	TOTAL LIABILITIES	$32.00
		OWNER'S EQUITY	
PREPAID EXPENSE	$2.00	ORIGINAL INVESTMENT	$5.00
FIXED ASSETS $12 $1	$11.00	RETAINED EARNINGS	$52.00
		EARNINGS WEEK TO DATE	$20.00
FIXED ASSETS	$20.00	TOTAL OWNER'S EQUITY	$77.00
TOTAL ASSETS	$109.00	TOTAL LIABILITIES & OWNER'S EQUITY	$109.00

Page 132

ASSETS		LIABILITIES	
CASH	$46.00	ACCOUNTS PAYABLE	$32.00
ACCOUNTS RECEIVABLE	$16.00	NOTES PAYABLE	$0.00
INVENTORY RAW MATERIALS $10 FINISHED GOODS $0	$10.00	TOTAL LIABILITIES	$32.00
		OWNER'S EQUITY	
PREPAID EXPENSE	$2.00	ORIGINAL INVESTMENT	$5.00
FIXED ASSETS $12 $1	$11.00	RETAINED EARNINGS	$52.00
		EARNINGS WEEK TO DATE	$16.00
FIXED ASSETS	$20.00	TOTAL OWNER'S EQUITY	$73.00
TOTAL ASSETS	$105.00	TOTAL LIABILITIES & OWNER'S EQUITY	$105.00

Page 133

ASSETS		LIABILITIES	
CASH	$46.00	ACCOUNTS PAYABLE	$32.00
ACCOUNTS RECEIVABLE	$16.00	NOTES PAYABLE	$0.00
INVENTORY RAW MATERIALS $10 FINISHED GOODS $0	$10.00	TOTAL LIABILITIES	$32.00
		OWNER'S EQUITY	
PREPAID EXPENSE	$2.00	ORIGINAL INVESTMENT	$5.00
FIXED ASSETS $12 $1	$11.00	RETAINED EARNINGS	$52.00
FIXED ASSETS $20 $4	$16.00	EARNINGS WEEK TO DATE	$12.00
		TOTAL OWNER'S EQUITY	$69.00
TOTAL ASSETS	$101.00	TOTAL LIABILITIES & OWNER'S EQUITY	$101.00

Page 135

ASSETS		LIABILITIES	
Cash	$46.00	Accounts Payable	$32.00
Accounts Receivable	$16.00	Notes Payable	$0
		Tax Liability	$3.00
Inventory	$10.00	TOTAL LIABILITIES	$35.00
Prepaid Expenses	$2.00		
Total Current Assets	$74.00	OWNER'S EQUITY	
		Original Investment	$5.00
Gross Fixed Assets	$32.00	Retained Earnings	$52.00
Accumulated Depreciation	$5.00	Earnings Week to Date	$9.00
Net Fixed Assets	$27.00	TOTAL EQUITY	$66.00
		Total Liabilities and	
Total Assets	$101.00	Owner's Equity	$101.00

Page 137

INCOME STATEMENT	Begin: Monday A.M. End: Sunday P.M.	
SALES		$50.00
Beginning Inventory	$10.00	
+ Purchases	$30.00	
= Total Available for Sale	$40.00	
- Ending Inventory		$10.00
= COST OF GOODS SOLD		$30.00
GROSS PROFIT =		$20.00
EXPENSES		
Salary	$4.00	
Depreciation	$4.00	
TOTAL EXPENSES		- $8.00
NET PROFIT		$12.00
INCOME TAXES (25% of Net Profit)		$3.00
PROFIT AFTER TAXES		$9.00

Page 138

CASH STATEMENT WEEK _____

COLLECTIONS	+ $50.00	
INVENTORY PAID	- $21.00	
INVESTMENT	-$20.00	
EXPENSES PAID	-$4.00	
CHANGE IN CASH (+50 - 45)		+ $5.00
BEGINNING CASH		$41.00
ENDING CASH	+	$46.00

ANSWERS TO CHAPTER NINE

Page 141

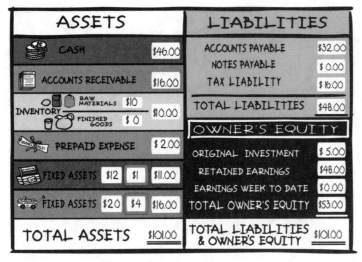

Page 142

Before Write-off

Earnings	Taxes @ 25%
$64.00	$16.00

After Write-off

Earnings	Taxes @ 25%
$54.00	$13.5 (round off to 14)

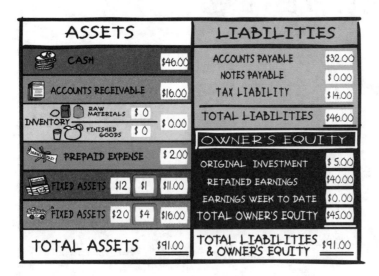

Page 144

ASSETS			LIABILITIES	
CASH		$18.00	ACCOUNTS PAYABLE	$0.00
			NOTES PAYABLE	$0.00
ACCOUNTS RECEIVABLE		$0.00	TAX LIABILITY	$0.00
INVENTORY — RAW MATERIALS $0 / FINISHED GOODS $0		$0.00	TOTAL LIABILITIES	$0.00
PREPAID EXPENSE		$0.00	OWNER'S EQUITY	
			ORIGINAL INVESTMENT	$5.00
FIXED ASSETS $12 $1		$11.00	RETAINED EARNINGS	$40.00
			EARNINGS WEEK TO DATE	$0.00
FIXED ASSETS $20 $4		$16.00	TOTAL OWNER'S EQUITY	$45.00
TOTAL ASSETS		$45.00	TOTAL LIABILITIES & OWNER'S EQUITY	$45.00

Page 146

FINAL ACCUMULATED INCOME STATEMENT   Begin: Monday A.M. End: Sunday P.M.

SALES (25 + 32 + 30 +50 + 50)			$187.00
Beginning Inventory	$0.00		
+ Purchases (12 + 4 + 20 + 20+ 20 +30)	$106.00		
Labor	$1.00		
= Total Available for Sale	$107.00		
- Ending Inventory		$0.00	
= COST OF GOODS SOLD		$107.00	
GROSS PROFIT =			$80.00

EXPENSES

Glass Rental	$2.00		
Advertising	$1.00		
Rent	$2.00		
Bad Debt	$4.00		
Interest	$4.00		
Insurance	$1.00		
Paint	$2.00		
Roof Repair	$1.00		
Depreciation	$5.00		
Salary	$4.00		
TOTAL EXPENSES		- $26.00	
NET PROFIT			$54.00
INCOME TAXES (25% of Net Profit)			$14.00
PROFIT AFTER TAXES			$40.00

Answers to Chapter Ten

Page 154-155

1. Yes.

2. Down

3. COGS

4. We had to buy lemonade at the store near the ballpark which was much more expensive. The real problem here was poor planning.

5. Better planning for purchases. The decision to buy the mobile unit and go to the game was made spur of the moment. Even though it is ultimately a good business decision, the lack of planning caused two major problems: 1) not enough cash flow, and 2) higher cost of goods, hence lower net profit.

Pre- and Post-Test Answers

1. B   6. A

2. C   7. A

3. A   8. A

4. C   9. C

5. A   10. C

Glossary

 ACCELERATED DEPRECIATION—A decline in the useful value of an asset which is more rapid in the beginning than at the end.

ACCOUNTING—Often called the language of business and is used to measure, record, report, and interpret the financial aspects of business.

ACCOUNTING EQUATION—Assets = Liabilities + Owners Equity. Accounting is based on the logic of this equation.

ACCOUNTS PAYABLE—Money that you owe to regular business creditors.

ACCOUNTS RECEIVABLE—Money that is owned to you from your customers.

ACCRUAL—Things which accumulate either as assets or equities. In accrual accounting, net profit is measured by the difference between revenues and expenses, not increases or decreases in cash.

ACRS—Accelerated Cost Recovery System.

AMORTIZATION—The process of gradually paying off a liability over a period of time.

ASSETS—In accounting, something of value in monetary terms.

 BALANCE SHEET—Shows the assets, liabilities, and owners equity at a given moment in time. The fundamental accounting equation of Assets = Liabilities + Owners Equity must always balance.

BEGINNING INVENTORY—The inventory that you have on hand at the beginning of an accounting period.

CAPITALIZATION—Costs that increase fixed assets and will not be consumed within one year.

CASH—Money in the till or in the bank.

CASH FLOW—The actual movement of cash within a business: Cash inflow minus cash outflow.

COST OF GOODS SOLD—Also known as Cost of Production. Inventory at the beginning of the accounting period, plus new inventory purchases, plus labor and other associated production costs, minus inventory at the end of the accounting period.

CURRENT ASSETS—Cash or other assets that can be converted into cash within one year.

CURRENT LIABILITIES—Money you owe that will ordinarily be paid within one year.

 DEPRECIATION—Reduction in the cost basis of the fixed assets due to wear and tear, passage of time, and obsolescence.

 EARNINGS YEAR-TO-DATE—Profit made this year but not yet distributed.

ENDING INVENTORY—The inventory that is on hand at the end of an accounting period.

EQUITIES—There are basically two kinds of equities (claims against assets): Claims of lenders or creditors which are called liabilities; and claims or rights that the owner has to the assets called Owners Equity.

EXPENDITURES—Same as capitalization.

EXPENSES—Costs of doing business other than those related to production. Expenses result in a decrease in owners equity. All expenses result in a decrease in earnings year to date.

 FIFO—First In, First Out. A method of valuing for inventory.

FIXED ASSETS—Property, plant, and equipment owned by a business. Things not normally intended for sale, which are used over and over again.

FIXED COSTS—Operating expenses that tend to remain constant regardless of variations in the volume of sales; for example, real estate taxes, property insurance, real depreciation on a building.

 GROSS PROFIT—Sales minus cost of goods or services sold.

INCOME STATEMENT—Summarizes the revenues and expenses of a company over a period of time, and reflects the difference between the two as a profit or a loss. Also called a P & L statement.

INTANGIBLE ASSETS—Patents, good will, logos, trademarks, and franchises.

INVENTORY—This is accounted for as raw materials, goods in process, and finished products.

INVESTMENT TAX CREDIT—An incentive offered by the government to encourage capital expenditures.

 LEASE—A rental contract.

LIABILITIES—Debts and accounts that are payable.

LIFO—Last In, First Out. A method of valuing for inventory.

LIQUIDITY—Ease with which assets can be converted into cash.

LONG-TERM LIABILITIES—Money owed that will not be repaid during the current year; for example, a mortgage.

 NET PROFIT—Same as net income. Gross profit minus expenses.

 ON ACCOUNT—If you are buying on credit, it is an account payable. If you sell on credit, it is an account receivable.

ORIGINAL INVESTMENT—Your own money that was used to start the company.

OWNERS EQUITY—This is the part of the assets that the owner has claims to after all the liabilities are paid.

 P & L STATEMENT—Profit and loss, see Income Statement.

PREPAID EXPENSES—Payments made in advance for which the company has not yet received the benefits.

PROFIT—"The Bottom Line." What is left over after paying all expenses, including taxes.

 RETAINED EARNINGS—The total cumulative net profit that a business earns over its life, and not yet distributed.

 STRAIGHT LINE DEPRECIATION—A method of allocating the net cost of a fixed asset in equal amounts over a set period of time.

 TAX LIABILITIES—Money owed the government for taxes.

VARIABLE COSTS—Expenses which are directly related to the volume of sales; for example, manufacturing labor, raw materials, and sales costs.

INDEX

About the Authors

Judith Orloff

For the past 25 years, Judith Orloff has been helping people transform their lives through self-awareness and education. Among her most significant accomplishments is the founding of the Burlington College in Vermont, where she also created a B.A. program in Transpersonal Psychology. In addition, Orloff is the founder of Educational Discoveries, Inc., which is the training industry leader in accelerative learning and instructional design. EDI is responsible for making The Accounting Game the most successful financial seminar in the world, with over 100,000 graduates.

Since Orloff became its CEO, Educational Discoveries has enjoyed steady growth and an expanding reputation and client base. EDI employs over 50 people and has 16 presenters and team leaders. Some of the most important organizations in the world, including AT&T, Kodak, Digital Equipment, NationsBank, Ingersoll-Rand, the U.S. Navy, and 3M, make up the clientele that EDI serves. Orloff lives with her son in Boulder, Colorado.

Darrell Mullis

Darrell Mullis served as the Director of Training and Development at Educational Discoveries for over twelve years where he taught EDI's learning technology and developed a training program for its trainers. Mullis has also taught over 300 of the phenomenally successful Accounting Game seminars to thousands of Americans. Mullis lives with his four daughters in Louisville, Colorado.